Dynamics of
Software
Development

Jim McCarthy

Foreword by Denis Gilbert,
Head Coach, Microsoft® Visual C++™

PUBLISHED BY
Microsoft Press
A Division of Microsoft Corporation
One Microsoft Way
Redmond, Washington 98052-6399

Copyright © 1995 by Jim McCarthy

Library of Congress Cataloging-in-Publication Data
McCarthy, Jim.
    Dynamics of software development : "don't flip the bozo bit" and
53 more rules for delivering great software on time / Jim McCarthy.
      p. cm.
    Includes index.
    ISBN 1-55615-823-8
    1. Computer software—Development. I. Title.
QA76.76.D47M387 1995
005.1'068—dc20   95-23189
                                                 CIP

Printed and bound in the United States of America.

1 2 3 4 5 6 7 8 9 MLML 0 9 8 7 6 5

Distributed to the book trade in Canada by Macmillan of Canada, a division of Canada Publishing Corporation.

A CIP catalogue record for this book is available from the British Library.

Microsoft Press books are available through booksellers and distributors worldwide. For further information about international editions, contact your local Microsoft Corporation office. Or contact Microsoft Press International directly at fax (206) 936-7329.

Apple is a registered trademark of Apple Computer, Inc. Jell-O is a registered trademark of Kraft General Foods, Inc. Microsoft, Windows, and the Windows logo are registered trademarks and Visual C++ and Windows NT are trademarks of Microsoft Corporation.

Acquisitions Editors: Dean Holmes, David Clark
Project Editor: Erin O'Connor

To Kevin, Danny,
Kelly, Alexandra, and
Fiona McCarthy.
Slender though it may
be, this is what your
father was doing.

———

Contents

Contents

Contents

Illustrations

—

Illustrations

Foreword

Imagine that Leonardo da Vinci, Tom Peters, and Robert Fulghum have co-authored a book on software development, and you'll have an idea of what to expect in Jim McCarthy's *Dynamics of Software Development*.

Jim's book is a visionary, animated, and pragmatic guide to developing great software, maybe even *historic software*, on time. Every time. Almost. More important, Jim's book is also about developing great software teams.

Jim McCarthy and I are partners. We work as part of a team that designs and develops software for Microsoft. Our software, Visual C++, is moderately successful by Microsoft standards. Hugely successful by anyone else's standards. Since we first shooed version 1.0 out the door a little more than two years ago, we've sold over a million copies.

This book is not about Visual C++, though, and it's not about Microsoft. It's about the lessons we learned while we happened to be working at Microsoft and happened to be working on Visual C++.

Even at Microsoft, which is arguably pretty good at building software, our team has a great reputation for hitting its dates and exceeding expectations. Whereas it's considered "OK" in some circles to routinely miss schedules—sometimes on the order of years—we're at the point where we do something that would've been unthinkable a few years ago, and that's still unthinkable for 99 percent of software teams: we ship software by subscription. A few years ago, our product release cycle was something like 12 to 24 months long. Today we're down to 4 months.

I personally guarantee that if you've ever had anything at all to do with software development, you'll relate to Jim's stories and see the wisdom in his rules of thumb. Jim's insight and advice are so perceptive, so appropriate, so right on, that you'll just *feel* he knows what he's talking about.

I also promise that no one will ever accuse Jim of taking an academic or formal approach to software development, or to management. This book comes out of the School of Experience, the School of Hard Knocks, the School of We-Never-Wanna-Lose-Another-Software-Review-Again.

Foreword

Dynamics of Software Development grew out of a talk entitled *21 Rules of Thumb for Shipping Great Software* that Jim has presented to standing room–only audiences around the planet. Altogether, tens of thousands of people have laughed, related to, and then applauded Jim's simple yet profound approach to building great software and great software teams.

Jim's rules of thumb, which seem (like Jim himself) to evolve and improve with time, embrace the whole of this business we love so much. It's chaotic, it's constantly changing, and it's limitless. Moreover, it's really fun. You get to meet colorful characters like Jim McCarthy, for instance.

But I'm getting ahead of myself.

I first met Jim McCarthy when he had but one rule of thumb: *When slipping, don't fall.* Or at least that's what he told me when I interviewed him in 1992. At the time, I had just settled in as the engineering manager for the now-defunct Microsoft Systems Languages group. Jim was from Whitewater and had been involved with the development of an early object-oriented programming language called Actor. What I remember most from the interview was that Jim was wearing cowboy boots. I remember thinking that this was the only interview I'd ever conducted in which both participants were wearing cowboy boots. Must've been an omen.

We didn't make our hiring decision solely on the basis of Jim's taste in boots, though, or on the basis of his single rule of thumb. Thinking back, I'd have to say that we hired Jim because he had another list in his pocket: *The Top Ten Reasons You Should Hire Jim McCarthy.*

That's what Jim does. He makes lists. Lists of lessons, lists of observations, lists of things that work. Over the years, Jim's pioneering rules of thumb have grown and grown, like Jack's beanstalk, into this Microsoft Press title and the most sought-after keynote talk on the software circuit.

Jim and I have shared some great adventures in these last few years. We share some of them with you in this book. Enjoy.

Denis Gilbert
Head Coach, Visual C++
Microsoft Corporation
June 1995

Preface

—

This book is my attempt to describe some of the dynamics likely to arise in the course of committed, long-term software development. The dynamics arose in—I'd even say dominated—the projects of my own experience that I depict in this book. As you might expect, the way I observe and interpet these dynamics has evolved over time and continues to evolve.

One side effect of publishing a narrative that contains factual, historical accounts is the likelihood that everybody involved in the events I remind them of here will remember and interpret the events uniquely. *Dynamics of Software Development* expresses *my* point of view. The emphases are on the aspects of the events that I experienced as interesting or significant. Here and there, I have changed a few insignificant details to provide anonymity or to highlight points I believe to be particularly important.

Any interpretation of an event or a series of events will inevitably, at least is likely to, gain depth and maturity with the passage of time and the acquisition of additional experience. It has taken me something like a year and a half of evenings and weekends to write this book. During that time, I've continued to learn about creating software. I'm sure that some of the dynamics and practices I discuss in this book will benefit from the deeper learning and more mature perspective I've acquired or will acquire since I first started to write about them. After all, software years are like dog years: one human year is equivalent to n software years, where n is proportional to the number of development milestones met (or attempted) in a single human year. Much software has been created while I was writing. Many software years have passed.

I have talked to enough developers and organizations to become convinced that the events I analyze in *Dynamics of Software Development* will be familiar to the many individuals and teams who are involved in creating both commercial and in-house software products. I hope that my ideas, viewpoints, and rules of thumb can constrain the risk and moderate the terror of software development uncertainty. I hope further that they can help create a framework for a definition of *software development normalcy*. Without a standard, broadly accepted view of what constitutes normal experience during software creation efforts, we are doomed to confuse the healthy and the pathological drives of the software team indefinitely, with no hope of remediation.

So there is a meta-point to this book: during a certain period of time, this is how the dynamics of creating software were experienced, interpreted, and to a surprising extent even managed (via a type of feedback) by a successful group of bright people devoted to shipping great software on time, many times. I believe that the insights and practices I describe have contributed substantially to the successes of the teams with which I have had the good fortune to be associated. I also believe that when I give it all a more reflective reading at a much later date, I will see this book's flaws as arising from the primitive state of our art rather than from sheer wrongheadedness.

Please consider *Dynamics of Software Development*, then, as documentary in nature. It might document a genuine stage in the evolution of software development or of a particular software development team, or it might merely document a singularity of both organizational behavior and analysis.

My hope, of course, is that *Dynamics of Software Development* contains threads that in later editions or further volumes can be woven into a more comprehensive tapestry.

Jim McCarthy
Redmond, Washington

Acknowledgments

I'd like to thank the men and women of the Visual C++ Business Unit (past and present) and its predecessor groups (Languages Business Unit, AFX) at Microsoft Corporation, from whom I pirated many of the ideas in this book. Especially representative of the team I've worked with are Jeff Beehler, Brad Christian, Greg DeMichillie, Michele Frame, Denis Gilbert, Jan Gray, Jeff Harbers, Kathryn Hinsch, Garth Hitchens, Eric Lang, Julie Larson, Perry Lee, Rico Mariani, Dean McCrory, Shirish Nadkarni, Andy Padawer, John Rae-Grant, Scott Randell, Keith Rowe, Steve Sinofsky, Steve Skrzyniarz, Clif Swigget, Manny Vellon, Audrey Watson, and Dave Weil. The many others from whom I've learned are too numerous to mention, but I would be remiss if I didn't mention Dave Moore and Chris Williams, intrepid evangelists, Microsoft-wide, for "best practices," both of whom were involved, at critical moments, with Visual C++.

The best ideas in this book come from these people and the people they lead. The worst ideas express my own pathologies.

I'd also like to thank Mark Achler and Chuck Duff, formerly of the Whitewater Group, and Bob Gianni and Tom Collura, formerly of Bell Laboratories, for their involvement in my software development career.

Erin O'Connor, the editor of this book, has earned my respect and my gratitude for her vision, her contributions, and her patience. And I'm grateful to Shawn Peck, who brought his considerable copyediting skills to bear on the pages when we had grown habituated to our worst gaffes and excesses.

Patrick McCarthy did great paintings for this book, paintings that are among the first I've seen that deal with the software development culture, the information culture. The illustrations alone can probably carry the book, should my words fail to do so.

Solveig Whittle went without a spouse for significant stretches of time during this weekend and evening project. When she did have a spouse, he was awash in guilt because he wasn't writing. The spouse in question owes her an enormous amount of everything good.

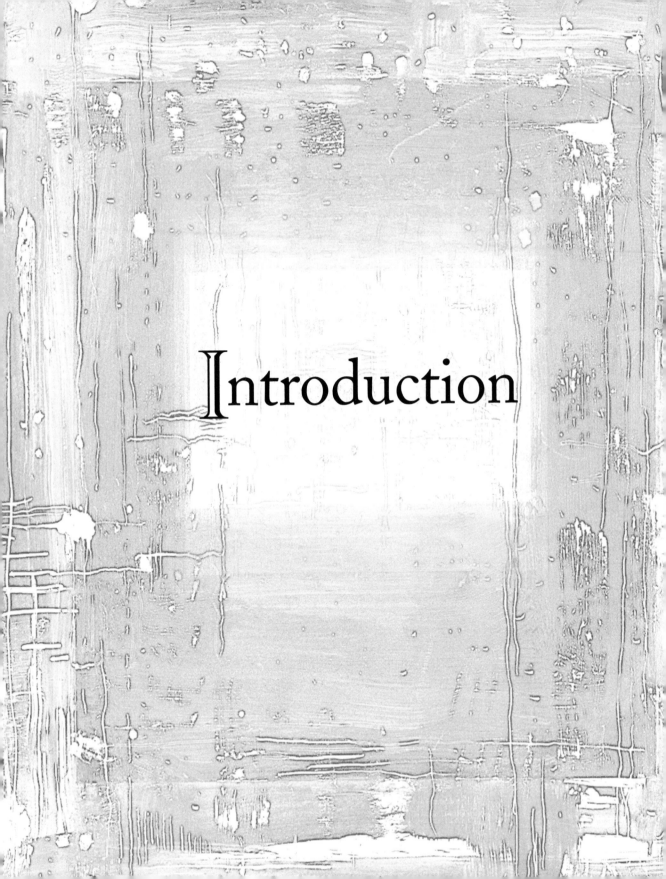

Introduction

Introduction

Shipping great software on time, the subject of this book, is a simple enterprise—at least at the conceptual level. First you develop a good understanding of your customers and of your position in the market. Then you define a software product that uniquely satisfies the market's needs. Then you develop the product and ship it, communicating its great value to the intended recipients. They buy it and are very happy they did. You are rewarded commensurably and take your place among the software illuminati. *Fortune, Wired,* and *Rolling Stone* do cover stories on you.

Of course, more people have ascended bodily into heaven than have shipped great software on time—which is probably why there has until now been no manual. And, of course, once you set out the magic formula, people will expect you to routinely follow it. Later on, I will have much to say about setting and maintaining expectations within your organization, but let me say right from the outset that shipping great software on time is the hardest thing on earth to do and that, although I want it to happen every time I come up to bat, no one can count on it. Shipping ordinary software on time is damned hard. Shipping great software in any time frame is extraordinary. Shipping great software on time is the rarest of earthly delights: you have the profound understanding of the customer; the requisite team in place, engaged and customer-focused; the product defined so that it perfectly hits the market sweet spot; the development process flawlessly executed; and then, pow! you launch the product to the oohs and ahs of a worshipful press. They mindlessly repeat the product's messages over and over. Ravenous hordes of money-toting customers camp outside the software store.

> **More people have ascended bodily into heaven than have shipped great software on time.**

Well, it can happen. And *Dynamics of Software Development* talks about several techniques that make it more likely to happen for you. Most of the techniques are cast as "rules of thumb"—memorable, pragmatic little maxims that can have a serious impact on the way you define, develop, and market software. Shipping great software on time is a difficult but not impossible undertaking. Elements you'd think would count the most count for very little. Development methodology, process, technical prowess, quality of tools, and depth of project management skills all influence the outcome of a software development project; but nothing will lead to success as much as the manager's ability to focus on the conceptually simple ideas presented in this book.

Making software is a multi-disciplinary task, and *Dynamics of Software Development* integrates suggestions for all of the software disciplines holistically. In my opinion, the creation of a software product is more a happening in the old sixties sense than it is a rigorously scheduled and functionally segregated project. This is not to say that I disdain organizing and coordinating the various aspects of software creation; but lurking just beneath the tidy, organized surface is a deep, rich psychocultural extravaganza, in which creativity, group dynamics, crude instincts, and technological fashion run riot. This chaos is where innovation comes from. It's where you'll find the greatness and the power of your team, which can be channeled via crisp organizational imperatives and encoded in exceptional software.

Lurking just beneath the tidy, organized surface is a deep, rich psychocultural extravaganza.

Think About It

Software is intellectual property, and creating software is primarily an intellectual endeavor. The bits on the disk or the CD embody the cumulative intellectual output of the software product development team. The more intellect embodied on the disk, the more intellectual property created and the higher the value of the product. With a higher-valued product, you can charge more money, get more customers, leverage your intellectual activity across a broader population, and produce other results of benefit to you and others.

If you focus your attention on the movement of intelligence from people to bits as the central activity of the software development team, you'll have a valid point of view from which to monitor or lead the development of software. Most software development managers or leads have an incoherent perception of the nature of the task they've undertaken. They think of their jobs as designing or coding or testing or documenting or marketing software or somehow "managing" the software development process.

Lateness is the usual result of such misapprehensions. Whatever else poorly thought through software development is, it is almost always late. Often the lateness is extreme, wildly off original estimates. Yes, the extent of the misestimation can make for some pretty funny jokes on the subject of vaporware, and that would be humorous if it were not so expensive in terms of dashed hopes, squandered money, wasted human potential, and lost productivity gains for society.

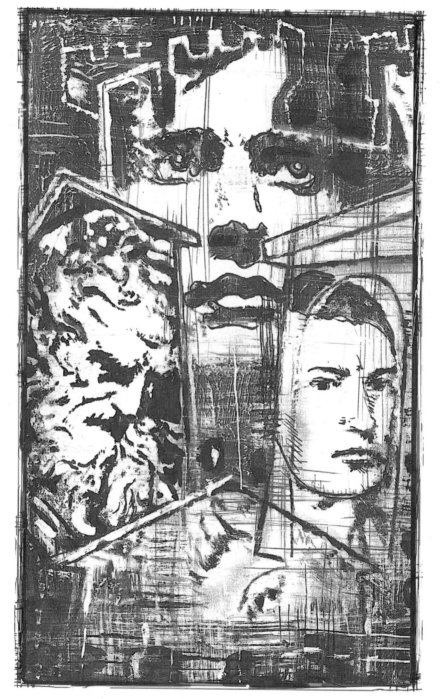

Intellectual Property

Introduction

The real task of software development management is to marshal as much intellect as possible and invest it in the activities that support the creation of the product. Intellect can take the form of abstract human qualities like creativity, cleverness, reasonableness, efficiency, and elegance. Intellect can take on other immaterial qualities like timeliness of availability and relevance to customer needs. The point is that to create intellectual property you need the intellectual involvement of the creators, and this involvement is the single hardest thing to achieve in any software development effort. Being on time, while not simple, is relatively straightforward for people who are individually and communally thinking about it. And producing even great software is within reach of the intellectually engaged team—and within only their reach.

Everybody's head has to be in the game if you're going to ship great software on time.

Assuming that sufficient financial commitments are backing the enterprise, the only remaining element that really counts is whether the team is fully engaged intellectually. All of the concepts and rules of thumb in this book are obvious to thinking people. They're common sense, really. In the main they address only three preoccupations: getting people to think, what people should be thinking about, and how to make people's thoughts effective. If you have ever been on an intellectually engaged software development team, you have probably discovered many of these principles yourself.

So what's the problem? If delivering great software on time is all just common sense, how come it is so rare?

Consider what the prevailing model of human endeavor has been. In most enterprises, you invest resources in two principal domains: intellectual activity on the one hand and rote mechanical effort on the other. You can think of these domains as design and production, or engineering and construction. By far the biggest part of the enterprise's resources (people and money) has usually been devoted to the mechanical effort. A car or a building or a highway has intellectual content to be sure, but the investment in engineering, while critical, is insignificant in relation to the total investment.

Now think about how you organize an enterprise that's largely mechanical in nature. The highest value is efficiency, and the organization of all elements stems from that valuation. Henry Ford secured a place in history as the "inventor" of the assembly line, the principal industrial process of the twentieth century. Repetitive, numbingly predictable, ruthlessly efficient, the line took in raw materials at one end and popped out tangible products at the other. Hierarchical organizations sprang up to feed and manage the line. Each person in the enterprise had a small, narrowly defined role.

With software, this ordering of affairs is rendered topsy-turvy. Where intellectual property rather than a tangible product is the desired output, the mechanical part of the effort shrinks dramatically.

Running the factory that produces the packaged software is surely not a simple undertaking, but it's probably no more complicated than running a factory that produces some other moderately complicated consumer good such as, say, mass-market cameras. And the real complications of running the packaged software factory undoubtedly arise from the uncertainties surrounding the availability of the "golden masters," the finished software to be duplicated. Given the intellectual content, the finished software, things can progress pretty smoothly.

The uncertainties and complexities of producing software are heavily weighted on the side of intellectual activity. Traditional organizational structures and mores are ill-suited to dealing with the migration of the central concerns of the enterprise from the mechanical effort domain to the gnarly world of scaled-up intellectual activity.

Articulated thought is the raw material of the intellectual product. But most of our commercial enterprises are not really designed to encourage thinking. You have to re-shape the enterprise a bit, or, in contemporary business parlance, "re-engineer" it. You need to figure out all the reasons people in your group aren't thinking and eliminate them—the reasons, not the people.

In this book, we'll try to capture the gestalt of a successful software enterprise, which won't parse neatly into discrete functional units. It's as important for the product manager to understand the fine points of managing schedule uncertainty as it is for the developer to fully comprehend the criticality of messages. And unless the individual team member has a vision for the whole, his or her contributions will necessarily be limited to executing functional scripts put out by his or her manager or a "metaprogrammer." This is a waste of human potential. Everybody's head has to be in the game if you're going to ship great software on time. Getting everybody's head into the game and keeping it there for the duration is the manager's primary role and is the running theme of this book.

The Stages of the Game

We can look at a software project as taking place in four major stages:

Opening Moves include creating a reasonable market strategy, a product design, and a development plan and undertaking the initial development activities. But the primary challenge in this stage—and what comes first in this book—is pulling together a functioning team amidst the typical chaos of a software development shop. The opening moves culminate in an event I call "Moving Day," the date on which the project might be said to have commenced in earnest.

The Middle Game is the (seemingly vast) expanse of time usually bounded at the early end by the first slip in the schedule and at the other by the onset of "Ship Mode." The middle game is roughly analogous in duration and travail to the forty years that passed in the desert while the god Yahweh forged a nation from a ragtag band of sporadically faithful refugee slaves. Usually the middle game lasts somewhat less than forty years, but the effect is often as if it has lasted at least that long. A bunch of survivors from the last project are somehow miraculously wrought into a group with a single-minded devotion to their overarching purpose: ship this evil software and bring this unholy misery to an end.

Ship Mode is what you must get into before you can get out of this hell. It's the only door. Like the transition period in childbirth, it's a time of pain and fear. And it's inevitable. You must go through ship mode in order to give birth. The only thing good about ship mode is the thrill of impending birth. The **Endgame** is the last excruciating, nail-biting month or so that culminates in the product's shipment.

Launch is that single climactic moment, the moment that will live on in the hearts and minds of your customers forever—or until the next launch, whichever comes sooner. With launch, the product is delivered.

If You Don't Ship Packaged Software

Dynamics of Software Development contains information that can still be extremely useful to you. The emphasis on packaged software products is arbitrary, derived more from my experience than from any fundamental differences between, say, commercial and corporate software development. It should not be very difficult to translate the principles I lay out in this book to the peculiarities of your world.

Opening Moves

Many books on software development describe project beginnings as if they took place in an ideal world. (This is true of descriptions of middles and ends, too, as far as that goes, but we'll debunk those assumptions when we come to them.) The team is presumed to be focused, rested, and in touch with the nature of the assignment. They gather requirements, create designs, and conduct iterative prototyping work; they solicit customer involvement and perform in-depth analysis of the technical problems posed by the requirements of the current project. Things are tidy, possibilities unlimited. Unfortunately, these presumptions aren't anything like the grim scene most of us encounter in the early stages of a new project.

And not only is the scene grim, but the challenges are horrific. The broad set of activities that must be set in motion in the opening moves of a good development effort spans five domains: the organization, the competition, the customer, the design, and development. Your opening moves are thus multi-dimensional and must synthesize your desired outcomes in all the dimensions in which you are playing.

The Organization

When I talk about the development organization, or team, I really mean the collection of people who perform the following functions:

Program Management—own the schedule, external dependencies, and manufacturing logistics; participate in design.

Quality Assurance (QA)—assess the status of the product; participate in design.

Development—write code; fix bugs; participate in design.

Product Management/Marketing—own the messages and the launch, the customers, and communications; participate in design.

Documentation/User Education—own the information required to use the product; participate in design.

You don't need to divide your team into these specific job categories (although it's generally most efficient to do that), but you do need to have all of those functions covered, with identifiable people held accountable for them. Notice that everybody participates in design. A unified and whole team vision is a prerequisite of great software. The minds of all the participants in the enterprise must be focused on the same thing.

If the people in these various software development disciplines don't perform well together (or haven't performed well together) as a team to create software, the very first thing you should do is work to develop an understanding of why the team is broken.

QA in a Ghetto?

If QA feels its charter is to test the product that Development has created—or Development is convinced that its job is to create a product that QA then tests—some alarm bells should go off. This common set of misapprehensions often results in alienation—elitism among the developers and a ghetto mentality among the "testers"—not to mention poor-quality software. QA's principal function—and it is a principal function—is to continually assess the state of the product so that the rest of the team's activities can be properly focused.

QA's ongoing assessment is integral to the act of software creation, not an *ex post facto* event. Naturally, a good deal of testing and analysis is required to properly gauge status, but the goal of QA is to support the product development process by providing an ongoing induction of reality. The value of this contribution can't be exaggerated. The unrelenting natural tendency in software development organizations is to transmute hopes and wishes into peculiar reality distortion fields. QA is a group's principal compensation for this nearly overwhelming urge.

Whose Design Is This, Anyway?

Or if any combination of Product Management, Program Management, and Development are fighting over who owns the product design, your "team" is goofy, looking for institutionally established authority, a weak substitute for genuine authority, which comes from having the best grasp of the situation. The goal in any

Some need for equilibrium forces people to behave narrowly, to specialize and to compete.

product design is that the best ideas become the basis of the product. Everybody should be working to achieve that goal. Conflict about which are the best ideas should be wrestled to the ground before the project commences. Design disputes can be readily resolved by gathering more information—referring questions to the customers via some sort of rapid turnaround, low-cost guerrilla market research. Or further discussion and the development of mutual understanding may yield a solution. Keen thinking will generally shed light on the problem that underlies the design dispute.

Usually in these quarrels over ownership, some need for equilibrium forces people to behave narrowly, to specialize and to compete. There is not "enough" of something, and the quarrelers identify with some function rather than with the product itself. The wise leader will interpret the quarrel as an expression of a problem that is somehow built into the organization at some level. Drilling down into the function vs. product identity conflict to discover its source is much more productive than dealing with the ownership quarrel as some sort of arbiter. Contrary to conventional wisdom, I have found that it's fruitless to clarify official ownership (although changing official ownership can be useful).

The issue of who officially owns what responsibility is not very interesting. In fact, it's a waste of time to try to sort out ownership. Healthy teams are composed of individuals performing in the roles to which they are best suited. This harmony between ability and role comes about because the individuals originally select their generic roles and are affirmed in these roles by management. Their generic roles are further refined and evolved to suit the circumstances of neighboring individuals. A team ecology, or system, develops, in which the boundaries of individual ownership are shaped by the distinctive capabilities of each person in the particular ecological "neighborhood." The system grows and achieves a balance and thereby becomes optimal with respect to individual roles. The team ecology is a natural phenomenon; no amount of mandating will have a positive effect on it. If neighbors fail to create among themselves sufficiently sustaining ecological roles for and with each other, the leadership may have to help analyze things. Clarification of roles "from on high," however, is hardly ever called for. Often it will become clear that an insufficient variety of gifts are present in a particular team neighborhood, so that people with similar gifts are struggling to occupy the same niche. The entire ecology in that neighborhood will collapse if management and the individual team members don't exhibit some flexibility. A collapsed (or unstable) ecology will mean that resources will have to be artificially imported into the neighborhood throughout the project.

In any event, before a project starts up, be sure you have identified the team areas that will need attention. The primary medium the software development manager works in is the medium of team dynamics. Just as individual team members are scoping out their work, designing their pieces of the product, and allocating their resources to their tasks, you, too, must be designing the teamwork you will be conducting during this project, and scheduling for yourself the particular initiatives you plan to conduct. Our first rules of thumb thus have to do with getting the team in gear.

#1: *Establish a shared vision.*

It might seem absurd to state such an obvious idea, yet the establishment of a shared vision is perhaps the most difficult feat of all to pull off. Everybody on the team must know what the team is trying to do, what the finished product will look like, what the basis of the product strategy is, and when they must deliver the product if it is to have its intended effect. Contradictory visions must be resolved and unified. A harmonious sense of purpose must be achieved. If it isn't, greatness is out of the question and even shipping becomes infinitely more complicated.

The techniques for establishing a shared vision range from despotic commands on one end of the management continuum to a survival-of-the-fittest, anarchic techno-free-for-all at the other. Before we look at a few of the techniques that fall in between these extremes, let's take a moment to consider what the contemporary concept of "vision" is all about. After all, having or not having "vision" seems to be a kind of litmus test for leadership these days.

Much has been said about the need for vision in economic and political power situations. Leaders, good ones at any rate, are expected to provide a vision to their followers. In my opinion, a leader's empathetic perception of the psychological state of his or her team is the beginning of what we call vision.

A wave of unity will wash over the entire community.

If the leader can then resonate with the team's complex emotional state—identify with it, articulate it, and give the whole constellation of feeling and thought a visible, concrete reality in his or her own personal voice or gesture—the boundaries among the individual team members and between the team members and the leader will collapse. A wave of unity will wash over the entire community. Empathy will be established: the leader and the team will feel and know as one, giving voice and identity to what was an incoherent psychological community substrate. And it will feel good to the team to be understood and to understand.

Often a sense of history, or at least a sense of the meaning of the moment, will inform the leader's empathy with the team. This sense of significance doesn't have to attach to history on a grand scale. It's most likely a sense of significance that attaches to the local history of the group, and to that history's relation to other local histories. The leader tells the team, in so many words, "We have been there, we are currently at this point, and we shall go there."

Shared Vision

But with or without a sense of history, this empathy with the team is what separates visionary leaders from demagogues. "Yes, we all feel this way and think this way," is the responsive cry of the team, "but what should we do?" At such a moment, effort, courage, and sacrifice can be summoned forth. The leader struggles with a straightforward sequence of questions: "What would these people do if they were I? How do I resolve their complex state of feeling into a clear mandate for action?" The answers the leader comes up with will determine everything.

The visionary leader will conceive of a future reality that must be created by the effort of the community, while the demagogue will perceive a need to remove something from the current situation. The visionary will harness the communal psychic energy toward a common goal, something that will require the delay of gratification; the demagogue will move to immediately sate the baser instincts he or she has excited.

Leadership and a group vision begin with the empathy between the leader and the team. Without empathy, vision is hollow, an ersatz vision that might fulfill a requirement that some words appear on a slide but that won't provide the visceral motivation that inspires a team to greatness.

A Tale from Close to Home

In the Languages Business Unit at Microsoft in 1992, circumstances were not optimal. The group had launched in April of that year the product popularly—or unpopularly—known as C7. The product had taken more than two years to complete, over many delays and a general deterioration into a seemingly endless death march. Microsoft's competitor had meanwhile grabbed the limelight by providing state-of-the-art tools for C and C++ Windows development. C7 was in many respects inadequate to the competitive threat. C7 did have clever packaging, aggressive pricing, an excellent class library (MFC 1.0), and Microsoft's traditional strength: the compiler generated quality code. These advantages would keep Microsoft at least marginally in the game, but it was clear that the next major release would have to radically reverse the negative trend.

Microsoft's C/C++ team had been deteriorating for many years, and at the end of the C7 project, management was changed for the third time in recent years. Denis Gilbert was the new senior development manager, and I was the new senior marketing and user education manager. Neither of us had had much experience in leading such a big team (over 200 people at the time). But both of us were very competitive and generally (though by no means always) willing to act. Jeff Harbers managed the AFX group, an elite team of successful developers from all over Microsoft who were charged

(continued)

with providing class libraries and wysiwyg programming tools for the C/C++ product. Their superior levels of experience were to prove invaluable, although trying to achieve teamwork from two such different development cultures was initially a source of much friction.

The Languages Group was the oldest group at Microsoft. Our first product had been Bill Gates's and Paul Allen's BASIC interpreter. The original languages business had been dwarfed as the company moved into operating systems and applications, and although Microsoft's relationship with developers remains to this day a core preoccupation of the company, its provision of state-of-the-art tools to developers had faltered for several years as the company's focus expanded into the other areas.

From 1992 on, upper management mostly pursued a policy of empowering us—or perhaps it was benign neglect, or even malign neglect! I won't try to analyze motives here, although I suspect that top management was mostly preoccupied with the enormous growth Microsoft was experiencing. This inattention at any rate made Denis and me especially accountable for whatever transpired on our watch, and we were acutely aware of that.

Among the events transpiring on our watch were a parade of bad reviews in the developer press, ridicule from analysts and customers, the derision of internal Microsoft colleagues, defection and brain drain, and a "goofy" management team, incoherent and without a vision. Everybody everywhere complained about our lack of vision. And if they weren't complaining about our lack of vision, they were complaining about either C7 or our inability to ship a product on time. The occasional e-mail from Bill Gates, usually along the lines of "you people in Languages are the stupidest people in the company," was—if not for the honor of receiving it—something we would just as soon have done without.

As we reviewed the myriad projects under way in our group, it became clear—primarily to Denis—that we were fooling ourselves in several important ways:

- ❖ We simply couldn't complete the work we had undertaken. We didn't have the capability.

- ❖ Even if we could finish everything we were building on time, we would still lose in the market. We weren't addressing the issues that came up repeatedly in reviews and in customer complaints.

- ❖ We had enough people and talent for one project, at the most two.

A Necessary Phase 1

Denis polled all the managers and the various leaders in the group, asking each to rank our projects. It became clear that everyone thought a single project, code-named Caviar, was the single most critical to our success. We concluded that if we could get Caviar out in good shape at the right moment, we would live to fight another day—and maybe even achieve a significant victory. The second most important project was code-named Barracuda, essentially Caviar ported to Windows NT.

All the rest of our projects, we decided, would have to go, and go now. We would be lucky to achieve these two. And, if need be, we would simply focus on one, Caviar. We would put everything we had behind shipping Caviar and winning in the market.

The simple exercise of listing all of our projects and then getting people to pick the most important ones yielded a "proto-consensus." It was not empowered consensus inasmuch as Denis was going to drive forward on this decision, not really soliciting a vote on further action so much as sharing his logic. We all saw that it was (barely) possible for us to win if we delivered Caviar, and we were willing to get behind that goal with as much capability as we could personally and communally muster.

Denis assembled the entire team, explained what we needed to do to beat the competition, cleared the decks of the improbable projects we weren't going to do, and announced a new organization.

That was the beginning, and it's worth noting that all of the elements that evolved more profoundly as we went on were present in embryo at the beginning: a consensus style, decisiveness, something clear for everybody to focus on, the potential for emotional gratification. Denis sensed correctly that the team felt frustrated and angry for not having been able to decisively beat our competition. He knew that the team wanted more than anything to win in the market even if that meant sacrificing individual pet projects. He felt that urge in himself and dramatized his feelings for the team by clearing the decks. His empathetic perception: "If someone would only make it possible for us," the team seemed to be saying, "we will win!"

Caviar would become Visual C++ 1.0 for Windows 3.1.

Having envisioned a world in which we won in the market was a tremendous boost for the team, although the complications of dropping people's pet projects in midstream did cause a fair amount of emotional turbulence. It was clear that Denis & Co. had created necessary but not sufficient grounds for success.

(continued)

Troubles Far from Over

The "team" had never before operated as a team. We had no notion of cross-functional subteams, and our eventual empowered consensus–style management was in its earliest, awkwardest, stages. We had no multi-release product plan or genuinely well-thought-through technology plan. We had no historically successful development process in place. Almost everybody doubted our ability to ship on time, even with our new clarity of purpose. After all, cancelling a bunch of projects and re-organizing could legitimately be regarded as the thrashing about of a team in its death throes. Only the results would tell whether we were developing or degenerating.

A few months passed, and it became clear to me that we were not going to ship Caviar on time. It was equally clear to me that we had to. We had decided to hit the ground running at Software Development '93 West, launch Visual C++ 1.0 with much fanfare, and have the product on the shelves—all before the competition could react. It was essential for our success, our morale, and our belief in ourselves that we ship on February 22, 1993, our target date.

And yet the development activity under way was chaotic. We were still adding features willy-nilly. We were doing some major performance tuning, which was good, but it was causing all sorts of global hiccups. We found it nearly impossible to build the product and had no repeatable daily build process. QA was a black box. Development would throw a release over the wall to QA, who would then spend several weeks testing it while Development raced ahead regardless.

At this point, approximately four months from our ship date, I was pretty alarmed. In one candid heart-to-heart talk, Jeff Harbers, the senior manager of the AFX group, pointed out to me that I would have to do something different if I wanted to ship this product. He got me to realize that nothing was stopping me from taking action except myself. I knew what had to be done, and yet for a variety of reasons, many of them personal, I held back. I was the director of marketing at the time. Although in previous incarnations I'd managed R&D for 15 separate Windows products, I didn't have that official job in the C++ group at Microsoft. Rather than risk "breaking out" of my pre-ordained role as "the marketing guy," I was standing by as we went down for the third time.

Harbers's gift to me was to get me to see that I was disempowering myself. Since I could see what a mess we had on our hands, he reasoned, I was responsible for it. There was no dodging my accountability. Although

Harbers was notorious for his unvarnished truthtelling, his truthtelling was almost always spot-on, and his challenge to me was ultimately motivating.

Denis and I discussed the predicament. Although we were uncertain of the precise diagnosis, let alone the remedy, we both knew intuitively that a significant change had to take place if the project were to succeed. We decided to call a team meeting for later that afternoon. This in itself was highly unusual. Assembling that many people with so little notice would get everybody's attention. We thought that if all went well this meeting would be the turning point psychologically for our team.

We'd cleared the decks of superfluous work, but we were still in dire straits in the market, losing in the reviews and with the customers, and we were sick to death of missing dates with mediocre products when we knew we were capable of so much more. We were within shooting distance of delivering a great product at the right moment if only we could pull ourselves together. There was nothing stopping us but us (and, of course, the unfathomable forces arrayed against anyone trying to ship software). The more I thought about these circumstances and about what they meant to us and to the company at this time, the more I found them personally motivating.

And I needed motivation, I needed energy, because I knew that we had everything we needed for success except a common vision. I had a visceral vision, of a breathtaking surprise victory for our team that went something like this: We would ship on time with a great product, Visual C++ 1.0. All of Microsoft would be pulling for us, especially the enormous marketing machine that had been neglecting us for fear of catching whatever ailed us. Our competitors, overconfident and expecting nothing from us, would be caught utterly flat-footed. The press would be blown away. We would in one moment of surpassing clarity and achievement reverse our decline.

My vision of victory was strong, but I was afraid to tell my colleagues on the team how I felt. Nobody was blocking me, but nobody had asked me to express myself on this subject, either. How I felt might be irrelevant to everyone else, even incomprehensible to them. My vision might be rejected as a ridiculous attempt to cheerlead. It was out of my bounds: "Who was this marketing guy, new to the team, to tell us what to do?"

But I hadn't moved my whole life to Redmond only to go down with bullets in my gun. I had to do something. So that afternoon I talked, telling the team how I felt and asking how they felt. I was sick of failure, angry at myself—were they? I was tired of having bad PR within Microsoft and outside, ashamed and embarrassed—were they? I felt Visual C++ 1.0 would be a great product, I was proud of it—were they? I thought we could ship it—did they? I was angry with our competitor and wanted to inflict a defeat on them—

(continued)

was I the only one who felt that way? I'd come to Microsoft to create tomorrow's world. If I didn't want to make a difference, I'd be working someplace else—wouldn't they?

I found the experience to be an eye-opener. Most of the team seemed to feel the way I did, to judge by their repeated show of hands and the way they seconded my remarks. Something happened at that meeting that unified the team by creating a genuinely shared vision: We'd ship VC++ 1.0 on time. Nothing else mattered. Everything would be invested in that simple, clear idea. Features would be sacrificed, other projects (even Visual C++ 1.0/NT) would be put on the back burner, no further energy or money would go into marketing C/C++ 7.0, resources would be acquired, the machines that were needed would be purchased—everything we had would go into this vision, and right now.

Following the team meeting, we simply asked every single group working on the product to contribute at least five practical ideas that we could implement right away and that would enable us to ship VC++ 1.0 on February 22. The "ship mode" section of this book grew out of the many wonderful ideas that flowed from the team in response to this simple request, but the point to note at this juncture is that the team itself had decided emotionally and psychologically to ship this product on time. They now had responsibility for telling the managers what they needed to achieve their goals. All the rest was straightforward execution. In the sense that Denis and I, at least, were going to do everything in our power to ship on time, including saying how we felt and instantly implementing numerous unconventional but practical techniques suggested by the team, this was in part a management-led vision.

I suspect that there is a critical moment (or multiple critical moments) in every team formation experience when the group emotions have to be embodied and articulated or dramatized in order to get the team to resonate with the vision and with the consequent universal, lucid sense of priorities. My purpose in telling this tale is not to aggrandize the Visual C++ team or its leadership (although they are a truly wonderful team and it has been a fantastic experience to be a part of their evolution) but rather to abstract and identify the elements that made a difference, at least in the psychological dimension.

First, someone perceived the problem and expressed himself. With his broader experience in managing teams on large software projects as well as his unique insight, Jeff Harbers could see that we were floundering. Although the steps we had taken so far were correct, they weren't enough. Even though no one asked him to or held him accountable (or, for that matter, gave him credit later), he decided to confront me about it.

The question of how to help someone who hasn't asked for it is a fundamental, complex, and recurrent difficulty in human endeavor, and, because of the personal nature of the work, it is aggravated when you're creating intellectual property. Harbers (although I've never post-mortemed the experience with him—he went on to other challenges after VC++ 1.0 had shipped) had to first know that he was correct in his perceptions, which takes a lot of confidence and is only the beginning of a big emotional investment. Then Harbers had to know that something had to be done and could be done and that he should make a large investment in fixing the problem, deciding that maybe I could be his leverage point into the team if only I could be made to listen up. Finally, in order to confront me, he had to "not care" what I felt or thought about him as a result. He had to risk his entire relationship, such as it was, with me and with the people I represented in order to tell me what he perceived.

His message hurt my pride, aroused my defensiveness, and made me argumentative with him initially. I was screwing up, he was saying, and I should be doing something differently. I fought his "help" with every intellectual and psychological resource I had. And he fought back without ambiguity or concern for my feelings. Still seething later, at 4:00 A.M., I remembered one particular admonition Harbers had given me: "Forget my mood," he'd said (angry, frustrated, cynical), "forget that it's me telling you this, forget pride and ego, just get the message."

Gradually, as I was able to detach the information he was providing me from the interpersonal and internal conflict I felt, my seething turned into positive energy. I realized that I didn't have to feel inferior to Harbers in order to exploit the advice he offered. I realized that I was being irrational and ego-driven. As I thought about what I could do with my new perspective, I gained access to my creativity and to an emerging courage to do something with it.

The lesson here is to *tell your truth* to people who don't perceive their problem or their potential. If you are wrong but open-minded, the team will correct your misperception of reality, primarily by giving you the information you don't have. If the team attacks you as arrogant or as a know-it-all, or says, who-are-you-to-tell-me, disregard their defensiveness. Point out to them that they are confusing your person with your perception and that the perception is offered in good faith. If someone says, "What, you're the only one here who knows how to create software?" you can simply respond that you're trying to offer something and ask why they don't want to understand it before they reject it.

(continued)

However the communication transpires, you have to be willing to risk your relationship with the team (and sometimes even your career or reputation) for the good of the team. If you aren't willing to take those kinds of risks, what you have to say won't be encoded with emotional content strong enough to break through the defensive walls you are confronting.

This truthtelling process is difficult emotionally and intellectually, but it is essential *a priori* for the creation of a true vision. Only the unfettered availability and convergence of multiple truths, with competition and selection among those truths, will result in the highest truth, in which the team will find their motivation.

Second, someone listened to a truth. The truth is hard to take, challenges your character, but whether the truth is offered by someone else or you discover it independently, you have to listen to it eventually. Insufficient confidence (where "confidence" really means courage) usually rules out your immediately accepting the insight. The perception might be stillborn, the creativity denied. All the varieties of insecurity can suborn your right instinct.

This is a two-stage process. Not only must you listen to the truth, but you must broadcast it to the rest of the team. And the medium for transmitting truth among humans, like it or not, is emotion. The only emotions you have unrestricted (if variable) access to are your own. This means that you must integrate the truth with the feelings it excites in you and transmit the combination to your teammates. Although you might be utterly rejected, you might also motivate the team and be entirely affirmed.

We were able to ship VC++ 1.0 on time. It was a great product. Microsoft's marketing machine did get behind us. Our competitors were caught flat-footed. The press did treat us well. We'd reversed our decline.

Our team gradually developed more orderly and less urgent ways to develop a shared vision (see Rule #3: "Create a multi-release technology plan"), but I don't think any has been as engaging, or as harmonious, as clear, or as gratifying as the vision we shared in the latter parts of our way to Visual C++ 1.0.

#2: *Get their heads into the game.*

If everybody on the team is thinking about the most effective possible behavior, the team's behavior has a chance of being more effective. Otherwise, it doesn't. This is another obvious truth, but actually getting everybody to think is a signal management achievement. If such an accomplishment comes to pass, it is only because thoughtful and skillful people have worked to create an environment in which it could happen.

It's difficult to overstate the value of coherent communal thinking, and it's easy to understate the difficulty of achieving coherent team thinking. Of course, everyone on the team has his or her own thoughts regardless of the cohesion of the team. And therein lies the problem.

People have thoughts, ideas, and beliefs, regardless of whether they express them. No, not all thoughts, ideas, and beliefs are worth expressing, but many of your team's are, particularly if you have hired smart. (See the appendix.) Almost all of your team's ideas are worth hearing. And associated beliefs are generally worth evaluating, too, especially if they are based on misinformation or partial information. People behave as they believe, changing either behavior or belief to maintain a semblance of consistency.

The Goodness of Ideas

In a creative environment, *the more ideas the better*. Simply encouraging "idea-consciousness" can have a profound impact. For people discussing a problem to realize that they are working with too few ideas, for instance, is a tremendous step. Every meeting should generate at least one or two good ideas per person in attendance. Keep count.

It feels good to have an idea. When one or more previously unrelated data points or thoughts combine into a new, more complex, richer, and more fruitful hyper-thought—or idea—the brain's pleasure centers get exercised. Creativity and joy are closely linked.

It's gratifying to have your ideas be listened to and understood. And it is one of the highest joys to have your idea become generally accepted. It's rewarding and validating to receive such positive acknowledgment of your mental processes. Your generating an idea is an intimate act, and when someone congratulates you or affirms you in any way for one of your ideas, the pleasure you experience can invariably be seen on your face. Usually, you radiate happiness.

Ideas are infectious. A truly good idea will spread like a virus. Everyone who hears it will experience some of the pleasure inherent in the creative act. This promotes bonding.

Ideas are multiplicative. Once underlying erroneous assumptions have been challenged by a good idea, other good ideas will flow from the same vein of thought.

(continued)

The Goodness of Ideas *continued*

Ideas generate the reciprocal attribute of critical thought, discernment, the ability to judge the value and the costs associated with an idea.

There is no downside to ideas. Cultivating the ability to generate a particular class of ideas at the time they are most appropriate can be difficult, but in essence, idea generation is simplicity itself. Your creative energy will almost always come to you when you summon it. Once it's on the scene, creative energy is like a fusion reaction, feeding on itself.

Why won't the members of the team think together and talk about what they think?

- ❖ They think no one expects them to.
- ❖ They think someone else is supposed to tell them what to do.
- ❖ They think that it doesn't do any good, that creative behavior is frowned upon.
- ❖ They aren't accountable for the disposition of their efforts.
- ❖ Managers view their own functions as directorial.

People will think and express themselves if their ideas have application. If their ideas are substantial enough to survive team scrutiny and emerge from the team as among the best ideas about how to proceed—that is, if their ideas are worthy of implementation—seeing their ideas realized will be a handsome reinforcement. I call this decision-making style "empowered consensus." I suppose there are better phrases, but empowered consensus captures the two processes I like to see applied to every idea before it shows up in our CDs.

#3: *Create a multi-release technology plan.*

The extent of your team's trust in the future will stem from their degree of happiness with their committment to and involvement in what I call "the technology plan." The technology plan is the fundamental output of empowered consensus, the basis of all trust in the future. In the rough democracy empowered consensus creates, everybody gets a kind of vote on the technology plan. More important, everybody's input is rigorously sought. The technology plan is the foundation of all team behavior: ideally, it embodies the best thinking of all the team members.

The technology plan is the contract among the team members, the constitution of the group. Updated once or twice a year, it expresses the communal intentions of all the individuals. This makes people relax. They can trust in the future. The technology plan creates a kind of Tomorrowland that has credibility. So, for example, if a team member isn't doing his very favorite thing on the current release, he can see how the next release might bring him a better assignment. Or if a team member doesn't like the direction in which the product seems to be moving, she knows that she can bide her time until the next update of the technology plan.

Having a technology plan is a great advantage in shipping, too. One problem in shipping on time or at all is that developers tend to have great technical ambitions. But if people trust in the future, they don't feel compelled to get everything done *this time*.

And the simple solution is easily understood. "Oh, yes, I understand how we'd do that."

When it's clear that everyone understands what they're going to do, it's in the product. The simple solution is another of the great unknown eliminators.

A Technology Plan

One time I was called in as an observer on a team (in a company not my own) that was creating a technology plan. The senior development manager of a major technology area in the group assembled her five direct reports. They decided to focus on a time period of five years. (Even two or three years ahead is incredibly far away in techno-time. I wouldn't advise going five years.) They then proceeded to debate the merits of the various technologies that were relevant to their world.

One interesting issue they dealt with at length was the state of disrepair one major piece of their technology had fallen into over the years. They weren't proud of it. It was brittle, buggy, and big. It was slow. Some of the code was more than 10 years old! It didn't reflect modern design principles. They had grown increasingly reluctant to even touch it.

I suspect that every development organization has (at least) one major piece of code so convoluted, hacked upon, inflexible, and recalcitrant that it frightens them. A chunk of code of this type gradually becomes impossible to maintain, or to add features to, and it greatly inhibits the potential of the team to create great software.

I call this debilitating syndrome "the software cycle of poverty": it's impossible to repair the technology by re-architecting it while simultaneously trying to ship it in its next incarnation. Who can afford (the team thinks) to

(continued)

invest an entire product cycle or two in cleaning things up when the effort will yield little or no customer benefit during those cycles? The customer benefit won't come on stream for several releases, when the greater flexibility and resilience of the code will have enabled the team to add more features and enhance performance without being hampered by the old code.

The deeper and more pertinent question here is, How does such a state come to pass? What kind of technology stewardship yields crud? Without your analyzing and remediating the underlying causes of the neglect and abuse that led to such decay, there is little point in making major renovations; things will just fall apart yet again. Don't build over again on the same cracked foundation that ruined your previous house.

On the team I was called in to observe, several new members along with the senior manager, who was also new, were going to take responsibility for the moldy technology. Not surprisingly, a new spirit of vitality and hopeful-ness arose. The team wanted to re-architect their troubled technology. They wanted to create more opportunities for themselves as technologists and for their customers as users.

The small management group working on the plan, however, leaned toward buying a spanking-new piece of technology on which to build their future. When they presented this idea to the broader team, the reaction was decidedly mixed. One group thought it was a great idea, that the mess was simply too great to clean up even though compatibility with previous versions was at risk should they buy something new. The other group felt that they were quite capable of cleaning things up "if management would only give us the chance."

Management was torn. The emotional side of the senior manager leaned toward giving the team what they wanted, toward letting them clean up their own technology, a technology they had struggled with for years. But a more calculating side of her was afraid that the team were fundamentally unready to take on such a monumental challenge, particularly after she'd examined their track record. She wasn't convinced that "management" was to blame, although she did feel that earlier management had been irresponsible in al-lowing such technological and organizational decay to persist.

In most organizations, if "management" requires sloppy work by exploit-ing rather than nurturing the technology, good team members feel it's time to move on. People who have no self-respect tend to stay, while those who have self-respect tend to leave. The team and the technology devolve in the same ways.

In this situation, though, there were sufficient new people (including the manager herself) to upset the equilibrium that had led to the long life of such poor technology. Perhaps what had been missing was the commitment of management to good technology and to the careers, creativity, and general welfare of the team members. The manager wanted to believe that her efforts could make a difference.

In the end, she risked her career on empowering the team, who not only revitalized the technology in a single product cycle but slipped in a few killer features to boot and deployed it on time! She also lost a few people who believed the team and the technology were unsalvageable.

The next time she updated her technology plan, the senior manager didn't convene a small task group. Instead, she trained her managers to facilitate the participation of the frontline team in the development of the technology plan so that the technology plan expressed the dreams and the wishes of the team who would be charged with its delivery. She also encouraged the other managers to facilitate discussion with all of the other software development disciplines that would be involved in the plan and with top management so that no opportunity for good ideas and consensus building would be overlooked.

There are a variety of ways to make a technology plan, but the most important thing is that there be one. There are several benefits to a solid technology plan. Perhaps most fundamentally, "throwaway" or "off-strategy" work is never unknowingly done. If you know where you're going, you can tell whether or not the steps you're taking are getting you closer to your goal. And unless you have a clear multi-release strategy, you have no way of knowing whether what you're doing will endure.

Refining the Technology Plan

The building I observed of another technology plan was a great example of empowered consensus. Scouts from both Development and Program Management were designated to rough-in design plans, which they did over a period of a month or two. (See Rule #5: "Use scouts.") The design plans were then circulated, commented upon, argued over, and ultimately bought into

(continued)

Refining the Technology Plan *continued*

by everybody who would be accountable for delivering on the plans, approximately 80 people in all.

Simultaneously, the plan was circulated to upper managers, who were collating numerous related technology plans into a coherent multi-release product plan. These managers didn't alter the plans at all because they knew how hard-won and valuable the consensus on them was; however, they did notice that the plans as submitted looked too much like long lists of unrelated features. How could big feature lists inspire the team over several releases? How could they explain such lists to the world? How could compact and potent marketing messages be broadcast around the world if they had to be based on dozens and dozens of features?

The managers noticed that the features could be categorized into five types: *strategic, competitive, customer satisfaction, investment,* and what they termed *paradigmatic* features. What they meant by "paradigmatic" was that the successive implementation of features in this category over a period of multiple releases would eventually *change the way people work*. This is not to say, of course, that paradigm changes were not competitively advantageous or a part of strategic thrust. Or that strategic features would not satisfy customers. But the managers did define precise meanings for each of the feature categories.

Strategic features were centered around fundamental and constraining choices. What operating system(s) would be supported? What object model would be adopted? What microprocessor would be targeted? What languages would be supported? Also into this category went particular initiatives that advanced the cause of their parent company in one way or another. For example, the parent company made printers for which they would provide special support.

Competitive features responded to or perhaps even trumped a feature that their competition had and they didn't. They didn't need to provide every single feature their competitors did, but if there were certain high-profile features that enraptured the press and their customers, they would invest in them. The number of features in this category was surprisingly small.

Customer satisfaction features were features they heard about all the time that their customers wanted. The least amount of listening to customers will yield a nice list of customer satisfaction features. The number of features in this category was large, but the cost of each was relatively low.

Investment features were those things they decided to do to their technology even though the benefits wouldn't show up in the next release (or even in the next few releases). It was axiomatic that any investment feature would have to enable a paradigmatic change in later releases. This discipline required the team to always try to get the most bang for the buck from their investment dollar.

Paradigmatic features, as I mentioned, were those that changed the way people worked. They were essentially an unreachable goal that the team would strive for with substantial features in each release. The marketing group would consistently proclaim in their communications over several releases the continued improvement and dominance the product offered with these features. These were also the features that would change the rules of the game competitively: if the paradigmatic features were successful, no competitor could hope to compete without matching them.

After classifying all the features into their appropriate buckets, the managers tried to decide what their level of investment in each category should be. They established what they felt was a good percentage of available resources to devote to each category, and then they tried to coordinate that level of investment with the technology plan's requirements. They were satisfied with the groups' internal allocations of resources. I'll leave it as an exercise to the reader to determine what percentage of the total should go into each category of features.

Then the entire team was assembled over a period of five days for two hours each day to review, step by step, the technology plan and in particular the plan for the next release. These five days (and the days immediately following) were the "final" opportunities for anyone and everyone on the team to voice concerns about the soundness of the plan. (Of course, plans can always change; this is one of the fundamentals of empowerment.) Because the plan had been originally created from the bottom up, there were few surprises. Because management had been able to aggregate features into a coherent story, the plan's purposes could be readily discerned and discussed. And because the entire process had been open and social, and the team fully empowered to create its own vision, the level of controversy was low, the ambitions high, and the enthusiasm noticeable. The team felt that it had vision. It did.

This is the best planning process I have ever observed. At this writing, the first major product to be developed under this plan is about to ship. It looks great.

A clear mission for the technology can be in everyone's mind simultaneously, and all new ideas can be bounced against the plan before more analysis is invested in them. The team members will be conscious of the extent of the work that went into the plan and aware that new initiatives will have to pass through a similarly extensive process. An idea therefore has to have considerable merit and probability of survival before it even gets submitted to the team for consideration. This tends to reduce random proposals and creates a relatively stable environment.

Finally, the categorization of the technology plan into strategic, competitive, customer satisfaction, investment, and paradigmatic features gives management a tool with which it can monitor investment levels and diagnose troubles. If technological leadership has been lost, for example, management can more readily prescribe new investment levels for paradigmatic features at the expense of features in one or more of the other categories.

#4: *Don't flip the bozo bit.*

I repeat. Software is intellectual property. You have to have intellects at work in order to get software. And the more intellects you have working at a higher rate of speed, the more value in intellectual property you're going to end up with. The obvious point is that people have to be thinking. Someone once asked me, "What's the hardest thing about software development?"

I didn't hesitate. "Getting people to think."

Believe it or not, most people don't want to think. They think they want to think, but they don't. It's easier not to and to instead flip the bozo bit—that's what we call it at Microsoft: "That dude's a bozo!" Then nobody pays any attention to anything the putative bozo says or does forevermore. And as far as his making a contribution is concerned, he's just dead weight, a bozo.

A bozo, of course, is not to be trusted with anything. The best you can hope for is that the bozo will be paid to do nothing of consequence and therefore won't screw up the works. This is, to say the least, too modest an ambition for anybody who occupies one of those valuable slots on your team.

Or you flip the bozo bit on yourself. You decide that you don't know what you're doing and that you're powerless anyway, so you become a dead weight.

We don't accept that sort of posture in our group. We get everybody's head into the game—anybody can contribute. Anybody on the team can tell you how to shave the time to market. Anybody on the team can tell you how you are going to slip. Anybody can. And you have to get the whole team thinking that way.

The clearest sign that people are thinking is that they listen to other people's ideas and critical feedback. They quiet their initially competitive responses to a possibly superior line of thought. They demand of themselves the intellectual rigor it takes to fairly and properly evaluate the new, potentially valuable information.

Don't Flip the Bozo Bit

They can filter out the ego-driven aspects of the communication they've just received because they can bring an understanding of human nature to a distillation of the true spirit of the message from the raw communication of it.

Thinking people can evaluate in the purest possible way all incoming insights. That they don't arises from two phenomena.

The first phenomenon, defensiveness, comes from the recipient's misunderstanding critical feedback. The act of creating intellectual property demands a great deal of emotional and creative investment. Criticism or better ideas about the product or the process of creating it get translated into criticism of the self. If the self were fully engaged in thinking, all would be well because on second thought the thinking person would purify the message, filtering out the ego-threatening and ego-driven aspects of it; however, that's not what usually happens.

The person who persists in pressing the ideas on other people is a bozo.

Instead of soliciting more information and developing greater understanding, the person on the receiving end puts primitive defenses into play. Head-on conflict or a passive-aggressive dismissal of the feedback or idea results, and no mature evaluation of the information ever takes place. When a single person repeatedly "assaults" another person with ideas or feedback, the recipient is faced with a dilemma: either the ideas and information are valuable (already dismissed out of hand), or the person who persists in pressing the ideas on the other person is a bozo. The recipient then sets the bit-flag on the persistent communicator: BOZO = TRUE.

The second phenomenon, even more common than the first, is the reciprocal. After her good ideas have been summarily and repeatedly rebuffed out of fear or other ill-motivated reactions, the communicator likewise flips the BOZO = TRUE bit on the recipient of her creative largesse.

Flipping the bozo bit is pernicious—costly, brutal, and nearly impossible not to do, especially when you are the one rebuffed. And once a leader has flipped the bozo bit on someone, people under the leader's influence will do likewise.

Of course, the remedy is to look within and make every effort to purify your part of the communication, whichever role you play in it. If the recipient is finding it difficult to accept your input, find a way to make it easier. At least explain your situation and your frustration. Conversely, if someone keeps giving you "bad" feedback or "lousy" ideas, look within to make sure that some primitive territorial defense isn't clouding your judgment. If you elevate this maxim to the status of a guiding principle in your group, people will invariably call foul when you or anyone transgresses.

Death March to Egghead

At the beginning of any software project, the team are usually just finishing up the previous project. If it has been an especially prolonged and difficult project (which almost all software projects are), this process of completion is affectionately referred to as a "death march."

When the endgame of the previous project runs a tad too long—say, a couple of unexpected months on top of several earlier slips—when the limits of executive ignorance and emotional stability have been thoroughly tested, when customers are howling about broken promises and the press is (or your colleagues are) snickering about your vaporware, that final exhilarating push to ship the project can deteriorate into a death march. In even the best of worlds, in which everything has finished up as expected (a key concept), the team are exhausted, physically and emotionally spent. Their beautiful imaginative design has degenerated (at their own hands!) into a shipping product. Ugly compromises have been made along the way. They know how many bugs they're shipping with. They know how deformed and inelegant the code is. There are huge expanses of brittle code that no one understands. They are afraid that it doesn't really work. Along the way, expediency has eroded their technical self-esteem. While they're not proud of that, there is a kind of pride that emerges, the pride of veterans, of survivors. They have faced combat and lived. In a project that has been properly load-balanced, each and every team member ends up convinced that his or her heroic personal sacrifices are what caused the product to ship. And they're right. Tremendous individual efforts, each critical, have made the difference.

There are huge expanses of brittle code that no one understands.

But now they feel they deserve a break, a reward, some R&R, and some opportunity to learn, to research, to play with what they love more than anything else, their computers.

The important thing to note is that, however they have marched, stumbled, lurched to the end of the previous project, the team have been perceiving the end of the previous project as the goal, victory, *finis*. This exclusive focus and determination is what got the previous project to the finish line at all. The team's intense preoccupation with the single goal of shipping is the only way any software ever ships. As the reality that there is another project looming behind the current one sets in, a variety of undesirable reactions set in, too. Burn-out (see the box), the most common expression of the individual software developer's ill-health, is the biggest immediate danger.

Burn-Out

As malaria was to the builders of the Panama Canal, developer burn-out is to the software world. Burn-out is when you just can't take it anymore. It's related to fatigue and also to depression, but it's specific to software production. Symptoms include

- ❖ an unshakable belief that the product sucks unnecessarily
- ❖ a conviction that management is incurably random
- ❖ feelings of nausea when contemplating the next release
- ❖ a cynical pessimism toward any organized attempt to solve problems
- ❖ wholesale flipping of the bozo bit—"That guy's a bozo"
- ❖ a lack of interest in computers (!)

PC Week and *Infoworld* (or *Dr. Dobb's* and *Midnight Engineering*) go unread. Science fiction seems silly. Virtual Reality begins to feel like AI all over again. A new version of MFC languishes unopened. The victim ceases to lobby for the current-model computer.

Managers, who might themselves be victims of burn-out, must take precautions because burn-out, while not virulently contagious, is mildly so and can infect a significant part of your team within the space of a few weeks or months if conditions are favorable to the contagion. The basic issue in developer burn-out is that the individual's passion, essential to producing great software, has been consumed or has become misdirected or is otherwise unavailable.

The role of passion in software development can't be overstated. To some people, the computer represents the ultimate in self-expression and self-discovery. As the pen is to the poet, the palette to the painter, is a compiler to a software developer. When the passion burns out, the compulsive interest in pouring oneself into an invisible yet coherent and dynamic stream of bits goes with it.

I joke about developer burn-out because, like all software developers, I fear it. Burn-out in a developer is the death of the artistic self, a perverse maturation, a shrinking with age, a withering with experience.

Burn-Out

#5: *Use scouts.*

Before you begin the next project, scout it out.

Scouts look ahead of and look out for the main body. They check out the terrain and its resources, find safe camping grounds, identify optimal routes, and serve as lookouts, watching for signs of the enemy. From time immemorial, whenever significant groups of people have been on a dangerous journey, they have sent scouts forward to check out the future. A software project is nothing if not a dangerous journey undertaken by significant groups of people, so send a clever person or two "up ahead" to scout out the next project.

> **Without someone to "make straight the ways of the team," you are doomed to wander around in the desert from one release to the next.**

The scouts can sniff around the state of anticipated dependencies—pending versions of operating systems, or other technologies you'll need or that will influence your next project—that will be under development simultaneously by someone else. Scouts can create or update the multi-release technology plan. (See Rule #3.) They can visit customers, get trained on competitive technology, make essential acquisitions, and lay out methods and procedures for the next project.

Scouts should propose minimum hardware configurations, analyze the resource requirements for all of the various development disciplines, prepare prototypes, and propose or confirm the validity of key initiatives for the next release. They should extrapolate from the difficulties the team is experiencing on the present project ways to address important issues in the next.

There is no end to the utility of scouts. Without someone to "make straight the ways of the team," you are doomed to wander around in the desert from one release to the next, going forward in disorganized and suboptimal lurches, if at all. With scouts you may very well still have insufficient vision; but without scouts you are surely traveling blind.

Looking Ahead

I recently met with the MIS group of a large company that had, over a period of about three years, successfully migrated thousands of their internal users from terminals attached to mainframes to networked PCs running Windows. As you might imagine, that was a complex undertaking, involving a substantial investment of people and money over a long period. And the organization endured a fair amount of pain as it absorbed this change.

Having achieved the deployment of Windows and PCs, the MIS team was now in the middle of a large effort to develop new technology that would exploit the company's modern, efficient hardware installation. The new, distributed, application they were creating would be the first big payoff for all the effort and money expended to date. They expected it to yield dozens of millions of dollars per year in new savings and profits.

The team was made up of approximately 100 people in the various disciplines, primarily in Development and QA, working on their new technology. Most of the developers and QA people were either new to the company or new to the technology or both. The company had never before developed a mission-critical PC application. Predictably enough, they were encountering a number of problems in completing it. At the time we met, they were several months late and significantly over budget, and a hard (and immovable) deadline was fast approaching.

From the time they had begun deploying PC hardware until the present, three years had elapsed. The new application they were developing thus targeted hardware that was already at least one generation out-of-date, on a network running an obsolete protocol, for an operating system that was now two releases out-of-date! The development tools they were using were two releases old, too, and still another major new release of the operating system was imminent. During the three years, hardware prices had dropped dramatically and the power of the installed base had risen as well. You couldn't even find their PCs in computer stores anymore. And now they couldn't get that first big application out.

I couldn't help but think that a judicious use of scouts would have made a difference. They'd reached many of their decisions, especially their software decisions—for tools and operating system—out of an innate and seemingly prudent conservatism: "Let's not change anything. It more or less works now." If they'd thoroughly investigated the degree of the compatibility problems they'd have had to face in order to keep up-to-date with versions— they'd have been minor—they could have seen that they could use the latest tools for their development and they could have targeted vastly improved versions of the operating system. The benefit they expected from their new application was so great that spending a few more dollars would have made sense. They could have determined precisely what they needed to do to maintain or boost their technological advantage rather than watch it wither away as they fussed and fretted with outmoded tools. They could have uncovered options they never knew they had.

This brave team of MIS people did finally get their big new application deployed successfully. Before they did, though, even in the middle of the career- and company-threatening crunch, they created two scout positions, assigning their most wily developers to check out the pending technological landscape.

I am generally sympathetic to the suffering of the slings and arrows of fortune that accompanies life in Edge City. The pace of technological change can ruthlessly overwhelm maladaptive organizations. There are technologies to stay away from; but there are also technologies to rush toward, as fast as dweeby little feet can be made to run, because they remedy critical deficiencies in technologies one has already adopted. Yes, picking up a "release 0" of anything should make you feel some trepidation. All other things remaining equal (or even improving), though, moving from a "release 7" to a "release 8" can spell the difference between utter catastrophe and techno-heroic triumph. If your decisions are thoroughly scouted, your plans well laid, and the dependencies understood, your willingness to change is your ultimate competitive weapon.

The basic idea, one I'll come at from several directions in this book, is not to slow the pace of change, or to create more stability; but to get good at change, at managing technology in motion. Dance is more beautiful than stasis. Movement holds more potential for adaptation and self-actualization than rigidity. Scouts are used only by a people that are under way, in motion, migrating. If you are standing still, you don't need scouts.

Using scouts can cause problems. If the scouts don't have a solid understanding of the multi-release plan, they won't really know what they're scouting. Or their initial reaction might be to regard the assignment as a "sandbox" assignment. They need to be sensitive to the enormous responsibility on their shoulders: one false pick of an OS or a tool, and the entire organization could die!

Of course, scouts can carry that sensitivity to their enormous responsibility too far, even unto an obnoxious self-importance. Sometimes the scouts disempower the nonscouts. If the scouts see their job as "defining the future," other team members might reasonably get their noses out of joint, feeling that they have no control over their own destinies. Deprived of the glamour, the power, and the pleasure of looking to the future, the nonscouts may also feel that attention has been distracted from where it belongs. They may wonder why all of the team's talent isn't being devoted to the nearly overwhelming task of shipping the current project: "I'm working 70-hour weeks while Mary is reading!" This resentment is especially pronounced when the most talented people, who could conceivably contribute the most to the current project, are scouting. And they should be.

Team members can be jealous of the scout assignment. It can seem better to be a scout than to be a developer—cooler, more "advanced," more "researchy." Being a scout for a few months (which is usually long enough) is a cool assignment. You get to see all the latest gizmos, meet with vendors and partners, play with prototypes, and influence the direction of the team's migration. But the scout doesn't design the next product. He or she does all the legwork in preparation for the consensus-building effort that is prerequisite to great software. If your team trusts that your commitment to a shared vision and empowered consensus is authentic, they will feel more and not less comfortable that their talented colleagues are hacking a path to their future.

As in other project team issues, the extent to which your team believes in the genuineness of your empowered consensus style of management governs the extent to which you can successfully use scouts. Whether or not you are destroyed by the onrush of technological change will therefore be a function of your commitment to the empowerment of every team member.

#6: *Watch the ratio.*

A common mistake many development managers make is to hire only developers, or to hire developers in numbers disproportionate to the rest of the team. The view seems to be that with more developers you can get more development done. If the objective is to finish the software project, this view is mistaken. Developers have a difficult time performing the functions of other members of the team. Skills are particular and grow as people apply them. Feet clap poorly, and hair curls better than noses.

In my group, the ratio is usually something like six developers, two or three QA people, one program manager, and two documentation people. The ratio varies all over Microsoft and will probably be slightly different for your team, too. But you are not going to get away with many more than two developers for every one QA person. The QA group are really the ones in charge of shipping the software. The first place we look when a product is late is QA. Are there enough of them? Are they adequately empowered? Did they get a vote on the design? Are they caught up with Development, or are they lagging substantially? Do they raise red flags promptly and efficiently? Are their expectations being met? Are there dozens of small "contracts" or handshake dates between Development and QA?

The real question when it comes to the ratio is not the actual numbers but the effective numbers. The healthy team will have an "effective" ratio along the lines described above; for example, you need two fully engaged, empowered people units (FEEPUs?) thinking about coding and debugging for every one fully engaged empowered people unit thinking about the state of the software. The raw number of humans can constrain the probability of achieving balance, but it can't guarantee it. Remember that the goal is balance.

#7: *Use feature teams.*

In the Visual C++ group at Microsoft, we use feature teams. I am unabashedly enthused about feature teams. They've had an amazing effect on our group.

If you ask a QA person from the Visual C++ team, "What's your job?" he or she will tell you, "My job is to ship the product." Not to test the product—that's a myopic view. The QA person's job is to ship the product. The QA person's job is to develop the product. The QA person's job is to design the product, to know the customers, and, in fact, to know everything that's going on in our technology plan, our product, our market, and our business.

We organize the development team—QA, Development, Documentation, Program Management, and, as appropriate, Marketing—in a conventional hierarchy, albeit a rather flat one (at least in the best cases); but we also take representatives from each of those four or five groups and put them into a feature team in a matrix organization. We take a chunk of the product, say, foobars, and tell the feature team, "OK, you are the foobar team." And they define the foobar as a team. They create their milestones as a team and articulate their schedule. They even define their process as a team—although we're always encouraging common processes across teams.

> **I can't recall a single case in which the feature team was overruled by management muckety-mucks.**

Feature teams are about empowerment, accountability, identity, consensus, and balance. They are the best mechanism I have encountered for remediating (over time) some of the organizational goofiness I described earlier.

Empowerment While it would be difficult to entrust one functional group or a single functional hierarchy, such as Development, for instance, with virtually absolute control over a particular technology area, it's a good idea to do that with a balanced, multi-disciplinary team. The frontline experts are the people who know more than anyone else about their area, and it seems dumb not to find a way to let them have control over their area. Although I can think of many bad decisions (and good ones) made by managers and overturned by other managers, I can't recall a single case in which the feature team was overruled by management muckety-mucks. I doubt whether at this stage of our group's evolution such a thing would even be possible. This says something about both the authentic power feature teams can wield and the quality of their output. (It also says a great deal about the importance of good hiring practices, and we'll look at that issue in the appendix to this book.)

Accountability One of the most interesting software development–related discussions I ever had was with the leadership of a feature team on the topic of accountability. The question we discussed was, "What are you accountable for?" My theory is that most of the best thinking in any group of humans is wasted, lost, because people who don't feel accountable can get into the neurotic ways of responding to new ideas that I talked about earlier, under Rule #4: "Don't flip the bozo bit."

First, the source—the person or group having the thought or the idea—might feel, "It isn't my area of responsibility" and so never say anything at all in a constructive way. The subsequent variety of pathological acting out of the critical thought can be astonishing. The "thought never spoken" gets enacted somehow, leading to all kinds of confusion, suboptimal behavior, and expense. Teams will vote with their feet if they don't talk with their mouths.

In that single gesture of asking for feedback, they disarm.

Second, if the source does say something (which is tremendously risky), the person or group at whom the thought or idea is directed (the target) can react defensively, and there are infinite styles of defensiveness. Sometimes defensiveness is quite hard to recognize, particularly in groups in which defensiveness has been identified as a negative value. Ironically, a more evolved group, one that has an ongoing consciousness of defensive behavior, simply evolves more elaborate and subtle ways to defend. Vociferous support of the status quo by the person or team responsible for it should always attract analysis.

Third, the source of the original idea might not stick with it until the idea detaches from the ego and becomes available to the target. Just as defensiveness is prevalent, so, too, is aggression. Usually the initial attempts to voice concern are all wrapped up in the built-in aggression and judgmentality that are nearly universal among humans. That triggers (appropriately) the defensiveness mentioned above. The target correctly perceives the aggression and, in defending against it, misses the "noble" component of the message. At this point, the source succumbs to its own aggressive pathology and dismisses the target as unworthy of further consideration and risk—that is, BOZO = TRUE.

Thus are many good critical constructs lost. The only remedy I know for this syndrome is the workshop. In a workshop environment, people voluntarily step forward and solicit the critical perceptions of their colleagues. In that single gesture of asking for feedback, they (more or less) disarm. This receptivity goes a long way toward nullifying to a large extent the aggressive pathology of the source. And since each person or group is a potential target of all the others, the ritual disarming pays everyone. I'm surprised that we don't use the workshop technique more frequently and more broadly.

I have successfully applied the workshop idea to real-world software development problems by promulgating the notion of "case studies" among some of the teams in my world. It works like this. A person volunteers to deliver an account of a case. The case, of course, is a current (or at least recent) professional and usually interpersonal situation in which the person is embroiled—for example, "I can't get buy-off for this idea," or "Nobody reads my mail," or "Developer X won't stick to the plan." The person talks for a few minutes about the case, sometimes changing names, sometimes not. The rest of the team then question the volunteer for more information and clarification—what steps have been tried, for instance. Then a somewhat prolonged discussion of the case ensues.

Two things about this simple technique never cease to amaze me. First, a plethora of ideas are generated. You can barely keep count of the times the case

One's own naked success or failure becomes painfully clear. volunteer says something to the effect of "That's a good idea" while scribbling furiously in his or her notebook. Second, the case almost always gets generalized. The rest of the team will say things like, "That's just like problem x I had last month." After enough similar cases have been mentioned, someone will say, "Isn't your problem really just a special case of y?" They will have identified the general principle or the general situation. Then all scribble in their notebooks.

Accountability offers lots of advantages and very few limits. If a balanced group of people are mutually accountable for all aspects of design, development, debugging, QA, shipping, and so on, they will devise ways to share critical observations with one another. Because they are accountable, if they perceive it, they own it. They must pass the perception to the rest of the team.

Identity Empowerment and accountability lead inevitably to identity. People identify with what they can control or influence. The higher the degree of control, the more the identification. While this kind of identification is generally good and is at least a prerequisite of great software, it can lead to situations in which gross individual pathologies express themselves in the product. An individual team member's self-destructiveness, for instance, might show up in the way he handles the function he identifies with.

With cross-functional feature teams, individuals gradually begin to identify with a part of the product rather than with a narrow specialized skill. There are very few competitors left to blame, and one's own naked success or failure becomes painfully clear. You can't go on blaming a management specter when all your encounters with management are of the kind in which management says, "What more do you need to achieve your goals?" You can't blame other functional areas when they are mutually accountable with you for all aspects of your feature. The question becomes, "What's blocking you?" In an empowered environment, the answer is inevitably something within.

Consensus Consensus is the atmosphere of a feature team. Since the point of identification is the feature rather than the function, and since the accountability for the feature is mutual, a certain degree of openness is safe, even necessary. I have observed teams reorganizing themselves, creating visions, reallocating resources, changing schedules, all without sticky conflict. The conflicts that do arise tend not to be personal and are generally resolved without recourse to management.

Balance Balance on a feature team is about diverse skill sets, diverse assignments, and diverse points of view. Because the team is composed of people representing multiple functional disciplines, it is diverse *prima facie* with respect to skills. Usually people who have specialized in one or another skill also have points of view that are complementary to their discipline. We can understand the diversity of team assignments by looking at the team's diverse points of view, characterized by the kinds of questions each team member type might be expected to worry about.

Program Management: What is the state of the team? How is the process going? How effective is our leadership? Where are we in the cycle? What is the quality of the schedule? Have the things we needed from other teams come in? Are our goals clear? What are we kidding ourselves about today? What list of things needs to be accomplished now? What is the theme of our team behavior this week?

QA: What is the probability that I will get the next handoff from Development? Where are we going with bugs? What types of bugs are we seeing? What functions are simply not there yet? How does this piece perform? Should I be raising any red flags this week? Does Program Management know how stable (or unstable) this piece is? How are our communications? Does everybody share a common point of view with respect to our state? What is the reasonableness of our stated goals for this week?

Development: What is the probability that I will meet this week's deliverables to QA and Documentation? Is this piece well designed? Will the user get it? Is how to use it clear? Is it fast enough, small enough? Have I fixed all the bugs in this piece? Is anything I'm doing or not doing blocking anybody else on the team? Do I believe in this week's goals? Is this work on or off strategy? Does it contribute to the technology plan, or is it a throwaway?

Product Management/Marketing: What will the customers think about this feature? How can I make the feature vivid to them in my communications? What emotional associations does this feature trigger? How could we intensify those associations by changing the product? How will the customers feel when they hear about this feature from me? When they first use it? Does this feature as presently constituted advance our relationship with the customers? What will the press make of it? What is the story behind this feature? Do I totally understand what the feature is and what its significance is? What is the probability of schedule success? Should I be introducing more uncertainty into the rest of the organization? Or more certainty? Where are we on the certainty-o-meter?

Documentation/User Education: Can this feature work any more simply? Is my explanation of how to use this feature utterly clear? Can we make it so that no explanation is required? So that the feature reveals itself to the maximum? If I can't write about the feature yet, is it late? Does QA think the feature is done? How does this feature feel to me? Is there any possible way to better it? Can I express myself more succinctly? Does the rest of the team buy into my writing?

Even though they're immensely valuable, feature teams can be hard to get together. Moving from a conventional hierarchical structure to the successful application of feature teams can be a very difficult transition. Several kinds of difficulties can arise from within and outside the feature team.

Inside the feature team, there will be a great deal of uncertainty. The feature team members won't know the limits of their autonomy. They'll feel that they ought to be working together better in some undefined way since management clearly wants them to be a "team," whatever that might mean. People will cling to their traditional roles. Developers will naturally be the dominant players at first. It will seem as if everybody on the team is playing his or her original role, with only marginally improved team communication. In fact, the cost of assembling the team, having a few meetings, deciding who is on which team, re-organizing the group, and so on will at first seem out of proportion to the benefit of marginally improved communication.

> **People think teamwork is equivalent to some namby-pamby consensus and bogus good cheer.**

People don't "get" feature teams at first. It's only as the inevitable failures start to mount up that the opportunities for bonding become manifest. Often a team will feel frustrated and abandoned as "Management" leaves the feature team alone to decide its own fate. This autonomy will produce considerable discomfort because people are unused to providing their own authority.

There will also be a great deal of conflict aversion, and this will be a continuing problem because most people's superficial notion of "teamwork" is that it is equivalent to some namby-pamby consensus and bogus good cheer.

The only consensus worth having is a creative one achieved in the combat of fully engaged intellects. Such a consensus is born of sleepless nights, fear of rejection, and trials of personal courage. Conflict, which usually presages growth, is the hallmark of such consensus.

But initially the feature teams are lackluster. The question of courage never arises because the challenge is to simply endure this latest management fad.

Eventually it will begin to dawn on some of the team members that they are in fact in power. No one is holding them back. Resources are available. Creativity is welcome. Management is there only to support their goals. They're within striking distance of the goals that started them on the course of software development in the first place. In a penetrating and even earthshaking moment, they realize that they are free to do and accountable for doing.

This creates another set of problems, of course. Many creative and brilliant people unconsciously insist that something hold them back, that some negative force prevent their gifts from emerging. They carry around within them a "governor" function that blocks the ultimate release of their full creative energy. This self-inhibiting stems no doubt from some early parental rejection of the child's beauty, passed blindly from parent to child, some introjected fearfulness of being: if I truly reveal my uniqueness, the child senses, you (the parent) will abandon me. Since few parents ever explicitly demand that their child limit his or her growth, we all tend to develop extremely subtle sensitivities that enable us to detect these negative parental demands. There probably is some healthy, gene-protecting impulse behind this urge to be "normal," to be the same as everybody else, to gain broad acceptance in the mediocre, average community, to conform to some homogenized value system; but this impulse is the antithesis of what is required for intellectual leadership and for the creation of great software.

Our self-limiting sensitivities—our compulsive search for negation—although healthy in a pathological environment become pathological in a healthy environment. We've attuned ourselves to perceive signals at every turn from our "management" and other authority figures that we are not to engage to the absolute fullest. And management might in fact be unconsciously putting out these "stop" signals (in the same blind and tragic way that parents undo their own children), but in the main, management at this stage should be (and usually is) a benign and affirmative supplier. At the very least, a good-faith effort is usually in place.

As individuals begin to "get" (and it is an "ah-hah"–grade experience) the fact that no one is opposing them and that they are accountable for their own success, they invariably transmit this notion, this feeling of liberation and empowerment, to others on the team. This personal liberation will be understood in varying degrees within a broad range of moments and manifested in a variety of ways, individual by individual. It's fascinating to observe. Each person needs to be challenged, encouraged, and nurtured. Flexibility and patience are demanded of everyone as people grow into their own awareness at their own pace. This growth process, however difficult, is a prerequisite of greatness in any intellectual team endeavor.

Bizarre conversations will ensue about who should be deciding what, about what the managers' roles are if not to control.

I've also observed that the degree to which people from a functional discipline (say, Documentation) will fully participate in the feature team is inversely proportional to their degree of success in the old, less empowered, regime. If a relatively functional team had isolated itself from the widespread dysfunctionality that had been surrounding it in the previous regime, and if it had been more or less successful as a result, the members of that older team will have a difficult time undoing their isolationist maladaptation when the rest of the organization grows healthier and it becomes safe to come out and play.

Outside the feature team, functional area managers (development managers, QA managers, manager managers, and so on) are meanwhile engaged in their own, often private, struggles. In spite of the lack of creative and intellectual teamwork in the overall group, they have succeeded as individual managers before "this feature team craze." To at least some extent, they will necessarily be opposed to the growth of the team. After all, they rose to positions of responsibility and authority in the unhealthy environment. They have been selected from the pool of available talent because they could achieve some level of results in spite of the handicaps

Managers Take the Helm

placed on them by the broader dysfunctionality. Now they are faced with the increasing irrelevance of their core skills. Their ability to empower themselves in a generally disempowered environment is no longer needed in an environment in which broad empowerment is validated. What has gained them success to date is now seen as a maladaptation. That which they were heretofore rewarded for becomes something they are penalized for.

These managers know how to ship software in a world opposed, how to get things done in an intellectual and creative ghetto. They watch the first tentative steps of the feature teams with concern, even alarm: "But they're doing it wrong. I should be doing this. I should just tell them what to do." These reactions come out of genuine concern. The temptation to take charge is nearly overwhelming. The senior manager will fear at first (I certainly did!) that the whole feature team thing may be crazy, that letting people with less experience and judgment decide the fate of the technology and the business is absurd, that they're making mistakes the manager has already made!

As the managers learn to walk the line between encouraging and teaching on the one hand and commanding and controlling on the other, bizarre conversations will ensue about who should be deciding what, about what the managers' roles are if not to control.

I experienced doubt. Several key managers were wondering what in God's name we were doing to a perfectly good team. I would wake up in the middle of the night, wondering why on earth we'd set out on this crazy jihad to get everybody's head into the game. We managers ultimately referred to this period as the time of our "Feature Team Angst." Gradually, we began to see that our role was to teach, to challenge, to encourage, and to add whatever value we could to the process. If our ideas were the best, they would survive. While the power resided in the main with the feature team, we could challenge their assumptions, get them to examine their motives and behavior, help them reach consensus and manage conflict, and articulate what we understood their vision to be back to them. We could coach them on their effectiveness. It was essential, however, because we wanted accountability from the teams, that we endow them with the power to decide and to act as they saw fit.

The only authority stems from knowledge, not position.

Of course, this entire process was gradual, and it is to some extent continuing to develop. There were many occasions when the feature teams basically demanded that management make some decisions or set some goals; likewise, there were some times when management inappropriately mandated something or other to the teams. It has not been a pure situation. But in the midst of all the change, I can occasionally catch glimpses of the ultimate organizational strategy for creating intellectual property.

In the ideal project, there are basically Creators and Facilitators. The Creators specialize in Development, Marketing, QA, or Documentation or some other directly applied software discipline. The Facilitators specialize in group cognition, in creating an environment in which it's safe to be creative and in which all the resources needed are applied to the problems associated with making ideas effective. The Facilitators make sure that the maximum number of ideas shows up "in the box." The Facilitators evolve from the ranks of today's managers and program managers, the people whose skills show up "in the box" indirectly.

The Facilitators are just as accountable for the quality of what ends up in the box as the Creators; and the Creators are as accountable for group cognition as the Facilitators. It's a good idea for these groups to be held accountable to each other, to be "reviewed" by each other in some fashion. The old hierarchy diminishes in importance. The only authority stems from knowledge, not position. This is a very challenging vision.

#8: *Use program managers.*

Program managers are the team members who perform the following functions:

- ❖ *Lead* the definition of a winning product.
- ❖ *Lead* the evangelization of the product's vision.
- ❖ *Lead* the team to predictable delivery.

It is perhaps simpler to define what a program manager is not than to describe the role more positively. The effective program manager is not what one is inclined to think he or she would be.

The program manager has little or no official power. At least initially, the discovery of this limitation causes the program manager a considerable amount of anxiety. The novice program manager will often think that he or she will be "writing the spec" for the product and that everybody else will implement, test, and document the program manager's grand vision in all of its revealed particulars. This is at best a naive view and at worst a foolish and destructive one. Before the program manager can be worth anything to the team, he or she must be thoroughly disabused of the notion that he or she has any direct control. Fortunately, in the healthy team, no one needs to take any special steps to see that this happens: the program manager's teammates will quickly disabuse him or her of any delusions of control he or she may be harboring.

Of course, this turn of events will cause beginning program managers some anguish and frustration. They will try to get their bosses to assert more control on their behalf. An inept boss will respond by trying to gain control on behalf of his or her little duckling, and this will trigger further goofiness. (See Rule #9: "Be an authority, not an authority figure.")

I have seen a variety of reactions to this initial disillusionment. The most common reaction is for the program manager to respond negatively to the genuine role of the program manager, which is leadership. This negation is generally cast as a rejection of "political bullshit." In addition to calling for an understanding of the dynamics of the technology, leadership in software development requires a high degree of sensitivity to the human nature of the enterprise, an awareness of the underlying drives

There is only a single moment in which "politics" is a legitimate "excuse."

and emotions that determine the team's behavior. Understandably, in order to avoid facing (and surmounting) a challenge of this complexity and magnitude, some program managers look for interpretations of their predicaments that will allow them to view themselves in the most favorable light. And in a community in which technical facility is the highest named value, it's superficially plausible to identify "politics" as the central bogeyman. This is also convenient inasmuch as mastery of technology is infinitely simpler than mastery of leadership.

And, in fact, what people often mean to do when they complain of "politics" in a business community is really to express their rejection of the entire miasma that results from incompetent leadership. Unfortunately, this miasma of institutional neuroses seems to be a more common environment than the healthier environment we are envisioning here. Often, perhaps even most often, it is at least partially accurate to blame "politics," in this sense of the word, for individual failure. However, there is only a single moment in which the "politics" diagnosis is a legitimate "excuse," the moment in which the program manager realizes that the environment is hopelessly unwell, terminal. After that single instant of recognition, the program manager (or anyone else) is accountable for his or her persistence in the unhealthy environment. What does it mean that the program manager or any other team members are choosing sickness? In this choice, they are supporting their comrades in failure.

Although initially many program managers are uncertain about their roles, insecure about their contributions, and scornful of "politics," when fully effective they wield vast amounts of power because all of their roles noted above are leadership roles. The program management group should really be an incubator, an academy, and a university of leadership in software development.

Program management is a technical track, and there are two aspects of technical mastery: (1) the technology with which the product is created and (2) the technical aspects of leadership in creating software, which is mostly the topic of this book. Program managers must master the many arts of cajoling, facilitating, inspiring, and demanding excellence and effectiveness from the rest of the team. They must know all the ins and outs of actually shipping software on time. They must apply the best practices that yield the definition of great products and healthy technology. And finally, they must be spokespeople to the team, to the press, to the customers, and to the corporate hierarchy.

Program managers are in the front lines in dealing with the group psyche. Program managers should be effective communicators and excellent listeners, and they need to have empathetic gifts. Program management is the heart of software development.

The Group Psyche

I want to introduce here a very important idea, to which I will return repeatedly. The idea is simply stated: software expresses the team that created it. Anything you need to know about the team can be discovered by examining the software, and vice versa. I highlight this idea because in my view it's the basis of software development management. The words and behavior of the team are really too confusing at any given moment to diagnose, but the software doesn't lie. The software will inevitably express every weakness and strength, every gift and curse, every unconscious ailment and top-of-mind brilliance the team possesses. When in doubt, turn to the software. You do have to be a bit facile with interpretation, in understanding how symbols emerge from groups of people. But if you are diligent in your study of the product, you don't even need to know the team to know what's wrong with it. Self-expression is irrepressible in the act of creating software. Ain't no lies in the box.

This idea is the basis of software development management theory. Without the software itself there is no second side to the equation TEAM = SOFTWARE.

The basic principle is, if you are having a hard time understanding something about the team, you can look to the software. If the team and the software both tell you the same thing, you can act on it with some degree of confidence. Conversely, if the software hasn't reached the desired state, the way to fix it is to analyze the genesis of the problem in the team.

I've said that TEAM = SOFTWARE, but what, really, is the team? What is the medium you're working in as a leader of the team? I'm convinced that the key to creating great software is to maintain constant contact with what I call "the group psyche." This somewhat Jungian notion is pretty abstract without elaboration; I see the line of argument and the practical application of group psyche analysis this way:

1. A collection of individuals are all trying to create a piece of intellectual property, a collection of ideas, together and simultaneously.

2. Individual creativity is mysterious, a limitless human power springing from the unconscious mind, enriched by the emotions, and constrained by the limits of mind and technical mastery.

The Group Psyche

3. That a group of people are wholeheartedly devoting themselves to a collective endeavor greatly compounds the individual creative mysteries. The creative mysteries become intermixed within the equally complex, compelling, and powerful framework of individual and collective relationships.

4. Leadership in such a situation becomes primarily a matter of interpersonal choreography.

5. That which validates and redoubles the creative impulses of an individual will scale up to the group, provided sufficient interpersonal skill is appropriately distributed among the group so that the requisite complex and highly charged feelings and ideas can be transmitted broadly.

6. Greatness, which is a superset of timeliness, will result from proper ministration to the group psyche. The group psyche can be seen as an abstract average of the individual psyches in the group. An individual psyche is

that part of an individual that enables him or her to feel, to think, and to reason.

7. Mediocrity, which is a superset of tardiness, will result from neglect of the group psyche.

Of course, the question is, How do you take care of the group psyche? The answer—from my experience at least—is this book.

#9: *Be an authority, not an authority figure.*

In organizational settings, many team members search for a kind of authority that isn't congruent with an optimally effective management style. This probably has to do with the need to re-create familiar power structures, as in a family, where the parents provide control and security and the children play a dependent role. Whatever the origin, the impulse to seek out this pattern of authority and dependence is strong, nearly overwhelming, and must be guarded against at all times—mainly because the manager's impulse will be to project an authoritative presence in response to the team's seeming need for authority.

The goal as far as authority is concerned is to make every team member an authority himself or herself. You want the team to have authority, both individually and collectively. That's where the manager's ultimate authority comes from.

In all social situations, people tend to cast the group into psychological structures with which they are familiar and comfortable. This is especially true of the work group. An individual team member will invest a lot of energy in interpreting the people (and the structures of people) he or she encounters at work as if they were groups and personalities with which the team member has successfully coped in the past. In particular, people tend to imbue their managers with the powers of their parents. The urge to do this seems universal, and in even the most enlightened people you'll find a nearly irresistible impulse to endow people "higher" in the hierarchy than themselves with the qualities of some sort of primitive power figure. This leads to all sorts of bizarre behavior and puts the manager in the odd position of fighting his or her own nearly irresistible reciprocal urges to become the power figure he or she has known in his or her own early history.

People tend to imbue their managers with the powers of their parents.

As in the family, the healthy team's encounter with authority evolves through three major stages: childhood, adolescence, and maturity. In the early stages of team formation, the childhood stage, the team see the manager as an omnipotent power figure, someone who decides what to do, secures all the resources, and is the source of all rewards and punishments—the caretaker and lawgiver supreme. The team members view themselves as having predetermined roles to play, roles predetermined by a succession of hierarchies. Because of their own beliefs about authority, the team members project a considerable number of ideals, of "should-bes," in the direction of the authority figure. "This is how it should be," they say, and then they go on to elaborate a simplistic and naive view of the relationship between the manager and the rest of the team. (It's worth noting, incidentally, that the team's projections of "how authority should be" contain many marvelous insights into leadership, authority, and achievement. The whole spectrum of views of authority is represented in the collection of these innocent views. The wise leader will waste no opportunity to learn more about each and every team member's built-in expectations of authority.)

The manager's responding directly and guilelessly to these fantasies, however, will lead to a stunted, childish team, whose members will have unhealthy relationships with authority. Keep in mind that the goal is to endow each person on the team with the fullest possible authority, not to rake it in for yourself. Imposing a "vision" on the team may buy you some time by stilling complaints for an interval so that real growth can set in, and it's an appropriate step in some circumstances. It's probably better to impose a vision than to try to gain consensus for a group vision in an immature group. You might as well ask a group of toddlers to sit on the board of their day-care center. There are advantages to be gained from imposing a product vision on the team for the short term, but inevitably one or more true technology and product experts on the team will come forth with the appropriate product vision. The vision the manager must truly believe in and effectively transmit to the team is one of right roles.

Empowerment

Although I long for another word to describe this state of being because "empowerment" has become so debased in contemporary usage, empowerment by any name has to be a central value in any group creating intellectual property. We often confuse permissiveness with empowerment. But enabling people to do whatever they think best is very different from enabling them to think and do their best.

And to empower someone is to enable them to be their best, is to free them from the infinitely varied kinds of blockages that tend to plant themselves in the path of accomplishment in the untended organization. Freedom is the cornerstone of empowerment, freedom to develop and apply judgment, freedom to think and say what needs thinking and saying, freedom to take risks without extraneously punitive consequences.

(continued)

Be an Authority, Not an Authority Figure

Empowerment *continued*

Empowerment is the result of teaching and learning, not of neglect and anarchy. For a manager to say to a subordinate, "This is your decision" is empowering only when the manager has provided and continues to supply what's needed to make a good decision—training, information, adequate resources of whatever stripe. Otherwise, such a delegation is really a dereliction.

If everybody is empowered, how are decisions made when there's conflict? This is really more a theoretical than a practical problem. In a properly empowered environment, the situation is not anarchic and confrontational but is meritocratic. As people become secure, they abandon much of the foolishness that stems from weak egos. Devoid of ego pathology, most design, development, and organizational decisions are pure resource trade-offs. An empowered team is capable of analyzing the pluses and minuses of all potential approaches and of optimizing in the interests of a particular shared goal or vision. There is no right approach or wrong approach. There is a continuum of trade-off among features, resources, and time.

Your personal authority stems from knowing how to create the team, to initiate its growth, to double and redouble its growth, while empowering the team with good techniques and procedures for creating great software and shipping it on time. Your vision is of the group psyche and of the product of the group psyche, and of how the two relate. Your goal is to be a genuine authority in these matters, not some bogus institutional authority that's just a lightning rod for everyone's authority hangups. Those authority hangups, those projections, are, however, the material you use to create legitimate authority on the team. The group's strong feelings and knee-jerk responses to omnipotent parental power figures automatically guarantee their attention, their interest, and their superficial respect.

What is legitimate authority? Knowing what you're doing, communicating what you're doing, and expecting the team to add value to your behavior and ideas.

During this childhood period, expect complaints about a lack of direction, no vision, unwillingness to make tough decisions, and so on. The best thing to do to initiate the growth of the team's authority is to focus on the shipment of a product. Hold yourself accountable for the timely shipment of a reasonably good piece of software. Get very hands on, ignore hierarchical and functional boundaries, and see to it that the product ships on time. Eliminate all folderol, and be single-purposed and utterly focused on the goal of shipping the product. This stance will tend to demythologize the authority images unproductively floating about in the group's psyche and will provoke the team to greater maturity. The message that will get acted upon is, There is a task to do here, and it has to do with making software, not with who decides what, who rewards what, and who punishes what.

The Competition

In any market, there are four fundamental situations:

- ❖ You are alone in the market.
- ❖ You are in a dead heat with a competitor.
- ❖ You are behind a competitor.
- ❖ You are ahead of a competitor.

In any of these cases, you need to make important judgments about the direction in which the market is moving, about the direction your competition (if any) is coming from and going to, and about what your intercept vector will be.

A Little Anthropology

Before we analyze the interesting characteristics of and advance appropriate responses to each of these four competitive situations, let's spend a moment considering the nature of the competitive experience. I'm sure a real anthropologist could do better, but it does seem to me that the organizing metaphor of a commercial competitive environment is that all activities are part of some larger contest. In this contest, there are the victors and the vanquished. Threats and dreams, fears and hopes, intermingle in the minds and hearts of the contestants. This emotional-psychological constellation can create an energized and intensely focused communal state of being that often yields significant or even heroic achievement.

Commercial competition evolves from a warrior ethic and is about blood lust. It's a slightly more refined stand-in for the primitive and nearly ubiquitous urge to conquer one's enemies, abscond with their property, and destroy their future. I say "blood lust" because competition involves creating a richer environment for one's own offspring at the expense of the enemy's offspring: the spilled blood of an enemy vividly expresses the end of his or her procreation, making more of the world more available to my own progeny.

Even without this notion of direct interhuman competition, the (relatively) rapid and transcendent development of the core hunter culture in human groups must have inevitably selected the characteristic of individual participation in successful group aggression. The successful aggression might have been against prey

Wolf Team

only, or it might have been a struggle for the possession and cultivation of land. We might conclude that the extant humans are the ones who had a genetic predisposition to successful bonding in the aggressive pursuit of an objective. We can call the fulfillment of this genetic predisposition "teamwork." The word "teamwork" suggests to many a "touchy-feely," weak-kneed benevolence and ineffacacious good will, but teamwork is really exemplified by the image of a vicious pack of snarling wolves cornering a young lamb. The remorseless wolves move in and make the kill with exquisitely timed moves, in a horrifying ballet of conquest.

Human group aggression is a powerful if not always an especially attractive impulse. To engage in a commercial competitive struggle is to give contemporary expression to human roles that have evolved over hundreds of thousands of years.

We might reasonably conjecture that the "gene for teamwork capability" spread rapidly because of its devastating success over alternative genes. Whole populations of teamwork-incapables were doubtlessly eradicated in the ruthless onslaught of the teamwork-capables. Shouldn't we assume that this eliminative process is still going on?

I make no moral judgment about this human trait. If pressed, however, I would be personally inclined to rate it very highly. Civilization, communication, love, achievement, fidelity, and loyalty, as well as cunning and imagination, seem to spring from this base root. The urges to overwhelm a competitor, to kill prey, and to take and hold the land show up in human activity, and we need to take them into account in the organization of any group production and in a competitive situation. The people in your group are people who have been (at least in part) selected evolutionarily because of their ancestors' contributions to group victory.

If we view the competition as an enemy (which is fashionable in business and reasonable, too, given the foregoing), we must view the market as the prey both we and our enemy pursue, or as the land, the source of richness for our business progeny. If we capture the market, we deprive the enemy and drive them to some other land or destroy them altogether.

It is essential to realize that competitors will emerge for any market worth having. If you're in a good market, sooner if not later, a competitive team will emerge and mobilize their group aggression against you in a furious assault on your market. Your competitors will struggle ferociously to deny you your objective, to force you to seek other pastures, to destroy you. This is in their nature as competitors as well as in your own.

The Software Struggle

We can put all of this observation at the service of the idea that you must thoroughly assess your competitive position before you commence each and every project. In the increasingly rarified air of the high-tech businesses involved in software development, the competition is a more personal, more intimate struggle than it was in business generations past. The creation of software is about individual thought and creativity, and the competition is often about individual intellects pitted against other individual intellects. It's also a struggle that shifts ground with much greater speed than the competitive battles of the industrial era did. In any new order, the early years are the ones in which innovation moves most rapidly. And because we find ourselves at an early moment in the information era, entire technology revolutions in individual software categories are taking place inside a year's time.

It's difficult to think of a single software market in which fundamental change isn't possible in a single, short-lived product cycle.

The Software Struggle

It's difficult to think of a single software market in which fundamental change is not possible in a single, short-lived product cycle.

The potential for instantaneous, worldwide marketing of information products is both new and profound. High tech moves to the accelerated beat of the breathtaking technology changes happening every day. The 1996 version of a product can be more effective and compelling than the 1995 version by an order of magnitude. And communicating the new, vastly increased value of the 1996 version to the entire world can be a matter of straightforward execution.

Once you've diagnosed your situation, you should always consider the classic moves.

If you don't wrestle every day with these kinds of thoughts; if you are oblivious to the radical and historical changes under way around you, especially those in the lives of your customers; if you don't persistently muster the courage and skill to undermine and supplant your own current technology by innovating around it, on top of it, and clear through it, then surely as God made little Apple IIs, someone else will seize the historical moment and capture the minds, the hearts, and the wallets of the people you consider your customers.

Obviously, there are limitless ways to respond to a given competitive environment. But we've reduced the competitive situations to four archetypal cases, and I'd like to suggest that there are "classic moves," as in the opening moves of a chess game, to make in response to each. Once you've diagnosed your situation, you should always consider the classic moves.

#10: *Alone? A market without a competitor ain't.*

You often hear that a given company considers itself without competition, that the features of its product, its distribution, or its positioning are utterly unique, incomparable. Of course, there are some cases in which this is true, particularly in nascent markets where (usually substantial) investments are being made, or in mature or highly specialized markets, where monopolies might be expected to prevail; but in general, valuing this kind of position is muddled thinking, for several reasons.

First, a mistaken value assumption underlies this point of view—namely, that it is good to be alone in a market. Some company might be bragging about the lack of competition they face, maintaining that this makes for a rosy future. I don't believe that's necessarily so. If a market is healthy, it attracts competition. Competitors usually help build the category by marketing with you the functionality that is common to both your applications. Competitors validate you and your customers. They create a market with you.

Second, it is difficult enough to lead a market when competitors follow closely, copying your most successful features. But they do thus confirm your leadership. To be all alone in the market truly provokes existential angst. If you are investing in creating new paradigms, you need benchmarks, points of comparison. Something needs to be happening elsewhere in the market. And if nobody else wants what you have, how valuable can it be?

Third, when there's only one player in the market, there is low consumer identification with the one player in the segment. While your company may be synonymous with the functions of your product in the minds of your customers, they'll have a hard time identifying with your technology. When there is no choice there is little personal identification. People identify with a product by choosing it (and defending their choice). If you are alone in your market, the approach taken by your product won't be validated by others as a legitimate choice. Superior ideas often fail because of their utter

> **It costs large sums to articulate even the clearest of messages to a broad segment.**

uniqueness. Every purchase becomes heroic, a "bleeding-edge" adoption. Although suffering together during an early adoption phase can promote a good relationship between the customer and the software supplier, more often it leads to customer disillusionment with the supplier before the market really takes off.

Of course, market solitude can be justified in the two situations I mentioned earlier. The first is the "nascent market" case. To pioneer and then own a new, dramatically expanding market segment is the dream of many a software entrepreneur. Unfortunately, the pre-existing conditions necessary for successfully pioneering and then "settling" a new market tend to make such an enterprise prohibitively expensive for all but the largest and most well-financed software concerns or those who have some lock on the target customer segment.

The problem is at least twofold. First is the problem of promulgating messages. New ideas are often complex and hard to explain. It costs large sums to articulate even the clearest of messages to a broad segment. Unless by some stroke of communications genius or by the self-conscious urgency of the customer need you manage to hit a "sweet spot," you are unlikely to see market cognition efficient enough to outpace your capital.

Second, the odds are stacked against your getting the features, schedule, distribution, pricing, and general communications all right on the first or even the second try. Successive approximations, too, will exhaust your capital.

Of the monopoly case, there's little to be said. If you have a monopoly, you'll know it, and you'll probably figure out how to maintain it.

Feature Shoot-Out

#11: *Dead heat? Break out of a feature shoot-out.*

In intensely competitive situations, particularly those in which market leadership is indeterminate, a feature shoot-out often results. The question of which software can perform which function with what degree of quality becomes the predominant point of product assessment. You'll often hear the class of features that develops out of this scenario referred to as "check-box items," features done only to satisfy some mythical purchasing agent or reviewer that your product is more "full-featured" than your competitor's.

This is a costly and inefficient way to compete.

In terms of the software itself, there are two principal techniques for breaking out of a feature shoot-out. (We'll ignore alternative tactics involving price, distribution, service, and so on.) One classic move is to out-produce your competitor to the extent that you seize overwhelming feature advantages. The goal here is not merely to leapfrog, but to do a double leapfrog such that your competitor won't be able to catch up in a single product cycle. This is the brute-force approach. The difficulty with this approach, of course, lies in the expanded complexity of producing and communicating the double leapfrog. And as it is loaded up with feature upon feature, the product will grow ever more bloated and brittle. Stabilizing the product will take more and more time. Sluggishness is almost certain to creep in as size becomes a disadvantage.

> **As it is loaded up with feature upon feature, the product will grow ever more bloated and brittle.**

When you take this brute-force approach, you depend on your competitor to likewise take the brute-force approach to competing with you. If you happen to know that your competitor is taking and will stick to that approach, and if you are confident that you can more than double your competitor's value features, brute force is worth a try. But it's not the preferred approach to breaking out of a feature shoot-out, and it won't result in great software.

A second classic move is to invest significantly in paradigm-shifting features. Do enough of such features that it will be unlikely that your competitor will be working in all of the same areas. Three is probably the minimum number of paradigm-shifting features that will provide this degree of safety. Once you make a breakthrough in the paradigm arena, your competitor will be forced back to the drawing board, even if he or she is momentarily ahead in the feature shoot-out. Concede the feature shoot-out, and go for the paradigm-shifter. It won't matter if you're missing a few features if you've improved your customer's working life by a few thousand percent. But make sure your paradigm shifters actually shift paradigms. If they don't, they're just more fodder for the feature war.

#12: *Behind? Ship more often with new stuff.*

Every failure is exquisitely unique, but it's common to see a competitive situation in which one player falls behind because they haven't shipped at a pace equal to the opposition's. (Actually, they can fall behind for an infinite variety of reasons, but "shiplessness" is usually the most pronounced manifestation.) If the competition has "lapped" you—that is, they're one or more release cycles ahead of you—your situation is precarious and calls for dramatic refocusing.

If the gods are liberal with you, you will survive to fight on.

Whenever you refocus, you incur substantial costs. You run the risk of randomizing your team, which can be fatal in any software development arena. However, when you are being soundly thrashed in the market, you are already suffering from a potentially mortal malady. The cure will almost certainly involve high risks, and, as with chemotherapy, the cure may seem worse than the disease.

Being behind is a debilitating condition to find yourself in. The press, customers, colleagues, and upper management are all aware of your deficit position. It feels awful, and the outcome is always in doubt.

If the gods are liberal with you, you will survive to fight on. But painful choices lie ahead. In particular, you must show the world (including yourself and your team) that you are not resigning. This is essential. Nobody will buy lame-duck software from a company that is about to give up.

Reduce your PR effort. Let the reviewers pan your stuff. They're going to anyway. Collect all your resources for the next event. You have lost a battle but not the war. If you withdraw from the field in orderly fashion, preserving as much as possible, you can still win.

Don't pre-announce. Although you'll be tempted to brag about software you haven't shipped in order to salve your pride and give your customers a ray of hope, don't do it. Pre-announcing is a treacherous game to play. Inevitably, it takes the bang out of your launch and the sizzle out of your product.

In your own mind, and within your team only, acknowledge the defeat. Don't varnish it. The lustre potential of a cow pie is inherently low. Understand the top few things wrong with your product, and move to remedy them at once. Then launch anew.

If you are suffering from unacceptably buggy software, you must of course fix the main bugs and re-release. This is almost always a serious drain on your resources. The effort that goes into making a bug fix release is enormous. Even so, try not to charge anything for the bug fixes.

I think the best approach to gaining (or regaining) a leadership position can be expressed in a single word: relentlessness. You must be relentless in your pursuit and relentless in your attack. The classic maneuver is to ship at a faster rate than your competitor's rate. The idea, of course, is to gain the confidence of your customer and to show your stamina and heart. If competition is a contest, the customers are the audience. They love a good fight, and they have the power to put their thumbs up or down. Keep getting up off the mat. Show them your qualities, how you behave when you're the underdog.

If you can get your team to a state in which they routinely outship their competitor, and the investment levels in the competition are roughly equivalent, you will ultimately win the market. Shipping is the hardest thing to do. If you're better at shipping than your competitor, you're likely to be better than your competitor at virtually everything. Timely, frequent shipping is the manifestation of well-being on a software development team.

#13: *Ahead? Don't ever look back.*

So there *is* a munificent divinity overseeing all, and as a result you find yourself confronting the difficulties of leading the pack and the opportunities associated with setting overall category direction. Complacency is your enemy now. Keep the following things in mind:

It ain't permanent. Someone is going to beat you. Who? How? When?

You gotta compete with you. Now is the time to triple your investment in those paradigm-shifters. Do more with each release to undermine the status quo—even though you're the leader—and then establish yourself as the leader of the new equilibrium.

Set the pace of change higher than anybody else can meet. As the market leader, you have the opportunity to set the category agenda and determine the cycle rate. Presumably, you're making more money than anyone else in the field. Re-invest it in consolidating your hold on the lead. Conquering is difficult, but ruling is more difficult still. Although re-inventing yourself and your category runs counter to your intuitive bent at such a time, keep in mind that if a competitor takes control of the pace of change, they will force you to imitate and to lose your momentum. Remember that product life cycles are measured in months, not years. With this kind of generational cycle, things happen quickly, and you must always move quickly.

Demonstrate to everyone that you're committed to your course by burning the boats.

Burn the boats. Continue to take big, ineradicable risks. Settle the new territory you've conquered. Demonstrate to everyone that you're committed to your course by burning the boats, precluding all thoughts of going back. This may mean not being handicapped by your installed base. Compatibility kills. Provide your market with sufficient incentive to move at your pace, and compromise on compatibility. Pull them forward, but don't let them go back.

#14: *Take the oxygen along.*

When you buy into the idea of developing software for personal computers, in particular software for Microsoft operating systems, you need to understand that you're buying into a way of life. The pace of change is breathtaking, like the pace of the underlying social and technological change. Doing analysis, developing a system, deploying it, and then going into maintenance mode is no longer an operative model.

The unceasing change in software is driven by the global pulse of new operating systems releases, which have become the central organizing element in this stage of the information revolution. Hardware, peripheral, software, and mass communications organizations are all cycling with major releases of Windows. This rhythm is not something that will let up soon. A techno-industrial heartbeat has emerged from the primordial technological soup we used to swim around in.

A steady industry heartbeat has emerged from the primordial soup we used to swim around in.

It's essential to the well-being of your organization that it respond aggressively to these regular international technical changes. Shrink-wrap software companies basically package their knowledge up into products. The product is the primary means of communication. To solve the current problems with a product, the customer gets the next one. This is an ongoing process, not a one-shot decision.

It's not so much that you want the next operating system release for its own sake, though that in itself is often quite desirable; rather, it's the accompanying technology that your product needs. And if you skip a release, your competitor may not. Your customers will no longer be able to integrate off-the-shelf components with your software. They'll miss the considerable productivity and performance gains each new generation of computer technology offers, and they'll suffer both the real and the imagined pangs of feeling technologically inferior and unfashionable.

Don't neglect to consider the power of fashion. Don't dismiss it. Search your own feelings about car model years or clothes or music before you relegate the notion of fashion to the irrelevancy bin. Factor the powerful appeal to your customers of a new start, with all the latest conveniences, into your plans.

Accept the Oxygen

The Customer

Most software business is repeat business. And this ongoing customer-supplier relationship is difficult to manage well. We won't consider here the simple case in which the customer makes a single purchase from a supplier, whereupon they mutually abandon the relationship. This "single-purchase" simple case isn't worth our consideration because as long as the core computer technology races ahead, our customers will need periodic updates from their software suppliers. The complexities arising from the "ongoingness" of the customer-supplier relationship are particularly acute in the case of software products.

The primary cause of this abnormal degree of complexity in the customer-supplier relationship is the fact that many of our software products are heavily used and profoundly known. Visual C++, the product I work on, is used by most of our customers more than eight hours a day. I daresay that our average customer (who is male) spends more waking hours living in the virtual world of Visual C++ than he does in his home in the real world. He spends more time using our product than he spends with his spouse and children. That's something to think about!

A secondary source of complication in the relationship is the fact that not only does the customer invest an enormous percentage of his waking hours in our software products, but the products themselves inhibit his potential. They gate his effectiveness by presenting him with a predefined set of constraints, which, though they do automate the task, also limit the customer's freedom of expression.

The Captive Customer

If you provide software to a captive audience, pay extra attention to this section's discussion of the customer. Your ongoing customer transactions are more, not less, psychologically and emotionally complicated than business conducted in a normal competitive setting. Your customers are doing something not unlike doing business with family members. This kind of business is especially problematic—and supercharged with meaning.

Among other things, you must compensate for your customers' lack of choices among several products and the frustration and resentment that that can create over time. You must get your customers to "choose" you in spite of their captivity, not because of it. And since their relationship with you is one institutional commitment rather than a history of successive personal commitments, you begin in a negative posture.

Even that task has been analyzed (more or less expertly) by the designers of the product. The designers are the ones who have defined the steps of the task and the order in which they are normally executed, selected the functions to automate, constricted the output, and designated which computer hardware and system software must be used. The target of the designers is the majority case. The designers try to create something that mostly satisfies the most customers. This state of affairs can really frustrate the individual customer.

So the customer, although he uses the product constantly, has little direct influence over its design. In this respect, software is like manufactured houses: drawing information from a variety of sources, the factory architect tries to abstract the general housing needs of a population segment. Most likely, the architect has no direct relationship with any of his or her customers. The producer is trying to serve a market, not a customer, which tends to deprive any individual customer of significant power.

This power imbalance is necessary, but it does create complication in the relationship between the customer and the supplier. True, the individual customer of, say, a software tool company doesn't often have the resources (the knowledge and time, for example) to create the software tool, preferring instead to focus on the development of his or her own application. But the infinite variability of application techniques in contrast with the bounded nature of most applications themselves adds to the frustration. Although people like to do things in an individual way, most software applications either require a particular approach or are at least more congenial to the user if a particular approach supported by the software tool is employed. You can easily extend this line of reasoning to software applications customers, who don't encounter much flexibility in the way in which it is most advisable to use applications in particular business settings.

I can't do without it, yet I can't do with it what I want to do.

Trying to build configurability into either the software tool or an application to compensate for individual variation can complicate the software beyond the acceptable range for large numbers of people. Although an unacceptable degree of complexity isn't necessarily an artifact of configurability, the two often go hand in hand because configurability is hard to provide and attempts to provide it often fail. There is a natural tension between ease of use on the one hand and ease of changing use on the other. Usually you can reach the broader market by tackling the ease of use problem. Ease of use is a hard problem, but it's substantially simpler than the problem of dynamic adaptation. This difference in degree of difficulty is most obviously apparent in those cases (the majority?) in which the ease of changing use requirement is simply added to the ease of use requirement.

So in a world where time and resources are finite, a producer of software must make choices about product features, choices that inevitably limit the product's utility to the customer. In time, one or more of the software limitations frustrate or annoy virtually all of the software's customers to some extent. The software "fits" well enough to be used day in and day out but not well enough to be truly gratifying to use. Over time, the customer's having to shoehorn his or her life into maladapted software can become very wearing.

I give lots of talks about software development, and when I get to the subject of software and the customer, I like to put up a slide that says, simply, "MOST SOFTWARE SUCKS." This usually gets the audience to laugh, and that often leads to applause, sometimes prolonged applause. Of course, on rare occasion, someone will take issue with this bald declaration, whereupon I am forced to admit that today's software is usually better than no software at all. That's why software is a multi-billion–dollar business. But talk about faint praise!

I buy software. I even love it (at first) just because it *is* better than nothing at all. But as time goes on, I grow to hate a particular piece of software as I discover its limits, which are substantially more numerous than my own, and arranged differently. It doesn't fit. Then, in the natural course of things, I change. And the world around me changes. The software fits even worse. It's a dog. I hate it. And I'm dependent on this ill-fitting gizmo. Update me, please! I can't do without it, yet I can't do with it what I want to do.

A Simple Purchase Model

Customers come to buy software products in several stages. In one—no doubt oversimplified—model, the prospective customer proceeds through several emotional-psychological states, more or less sequentially. Usually the customer is first *attentive* to communications about the product. The customer then becomes *interested* in learning more about the product, ultimately becoming *convinced* that deciding to buy the product is an appropriate purchase decision. Naturally, if the customer refuses to pay attention, he or she can't possibly become interested. And if there's no interest, becoming convinced is out of the question. But even if the customer gets to the convinced stage, he or she is still not ready to buy. The customer must finally *desire* your product. Then, and only then, will the customer go through with a transaction.

You must design desirability into the product from the start. Then you must esthetically transmit the product's intrinsic desirability in all of your communications about it. Desire is an emotional state, the anticipation of joy, a bittersweet gladness at the prospect of gratified need.

This necessary sequence of emotional states means that the customer's need must be identified from the start. Imagine and identify the few properties of the software that will gratify the need—say, speed, for one. Visualize the properties, desire them yourself, and everywhere ensure and intensify their presence. Compromise individual functions rather than these central properties. Meditate on the nature of the properties you've identified, and evaluate the versions of your design in their light. Your focus should be on coaxing more of these central properties into every reachable nook of the program. Don't be satisfied until these qualities will be readily discerned and acutely felt. You want the most naive user to react to them, even to name them.

Esthetics

It's worth a brief digression here to talk about esthetics. Many people will have a passing familiarity with the term, but for most it will be a somewhat foggy notion, having to do with design and art in a general sort of way. A simple way to grasp what esthetics are is to consider the opposite: anesthetics, those things that render people insensible, that put them to sleep. The esthetic experience has the opposite effect, awakening people and sharpening their senses, bringing them to more, not less, consciousness.

And what are those things that awaken people? They're the sensible things—motion, balance, color, sound, shape—qualities that transparently manipulate perceptual forces in the customer, drawing him or her into the world of the software with the least effort of attention. Esthetically pleasing software is constructed with foresight and insight into the mental model it will provoke in the customer and with a complete consciousness at design time of the customer's likely perceptual state at all conceivable phases of the product's use.

The esthetic awakening, although physiologically based, transcends the physical. It creates a new sensibility, a new awareness of potential.

#15: *Enrapture the customer.*

Since most business is renewal business, with customers buying multiple releases over a relatively long period of time, the market has a deep understanding of your software and its flaws. And since the state of your organization is expressed in your product and the communications and services surrounding it, the market has a good sense of your organization and its flaws, too. Your customers *know* you.

If your customers have grown uncomfortably dependent on software that doesn't quite meet their needs (and that's typical), if they're spending hours every day uncomfortably shoehorning their lives into your product, they have come to crave your understanding and will respond enthusiastically to the least sign of it.

Normal success, meeting customer expectations, means speaking to the most outrageous and flagrant violations of the customer's needs from version to version.

The customer's least hope is that you'll understand his or her most excruciating experiences with your product.

Customers are likely to stay with you if you are faithful about that (although the fact that they're not mutinous doesn't mean that they won't be sullen). If a common transaction in your system is seriously cumbersome, for example, simplifying it somewhat in the next release will meet customer expectations. The customer's least hope is that you'll understand his or her most excruciating experiences with your product and that you'll express this understanding in the next release.

Great software, however, requires much more than normal success. For great software, you must pivot your entire technology so that it flows in the direction of the customers' deepest needs, not their least hopes. You must innovate in ways that clearly affirm their inarticulate desires, that show you really understand them. Surprise the customer by articulating and answering in your product concerns and fantasies that heretofore had been rumbling about in the customer's preconscious. Fix outrageous uglinesses, yes; but take the customer somewhere altogether new and fitting.

The fantasies of the market are generally centered on issues of empowerment, control, and security. The market wants to be able to do things with its computers that it currently can't. Customers often find they can't even publicly admit these needs for fear of appearing to be computer illiterate. They derive value and security from being able to apply your software to their needs. To admit that they can't do what they want to do requires a sense of security beyond most people's reach.

Market understanding is the foundation of great software. To repeatedly demonstrate through a series of two or three releases that you genuinely understand the market will result in enormous customer loyalty and brand equity. You will be viewed as the source of your customers' empowerment. They will be rapturous.

The question naturally arises, How do you find out what's annoying the customers? And more significant, How do you uncover their deepest needs? Put most simply, the answer is, You ask them. Anywhere and everywhere, in any style, in any medium.

A statistically valid picture of the market and its needs, so that market preferences are rendered inarguable and what your next product should be becomes obvious as a result of your statistical investigations, is difficult and expensive to achieve. If instead you're willing to live with the fact that relationship building is more an art than a science and that the important thing is that you listen, you'll have a relatively easy and inexpensive path to an understanding of the customer.

As the ads say, Just do it. Send letters out to some of your customers asking them what they like and dislike. Call them. Talk to them at trade shows. Run focus groups. None of this needs to be overwhelmingly complex or expensive. For a focus group, just rent a room somewhere, invite a bunch of local customers, and talk away. Write up your notes, and distribute them to the team. For a survey, ask your team if there's anything they want to know. If they have questions about the customers, put them in the survey. (If they don't, determine why your team is so lethargic.) Then just mail out the survey and communicate its results broadly.

You're not after precise accuracy so much as you're inculcating a set of values in your team that you can promulgate to your customers. In the lively team, everyone will argue about what the results of any customer listening exercise mean or don't mean. This is normal and good. Encourage it. Follow up those questions with the customers. Then argue about what those results mean. Build an evolving image of the market that becomes increasingly sophisticated. The process of knowing the customer is ongoing, not an expensive one-time market research project.

Gaining this understanding and embodying it in your software requires skill, creativity, and tenacity. You must recognize the central market need and organize all your technology and communications efforts in the direction of satisfying that need. Addressing the central need in your product will have these effects:

❖ Your product will appeal to the customer's sense of security.

❖ Your product will extend the customer's control.

❖ If all else were dropped from your product but the central need was met in unique ways, the product would be compelling.

❖ Your product messages will be clarified.

❖ Your product's use will be simplified.

#16: *Find the sweet spot.*

I believe that every market at all times has a sweet spot, a point of intersecting values. The sweet spot always moves (or evolves) as the market itself grows, sometimes rapidly, but if a product soundly strikes that sweet spot by incorporating those intersecting values, it will (when properly launched) take off as if of its own accord.

When we were creating Visual C++ 1.0, for example, the C++ market was only in its infancy, although the conventional wisdom had it that the market was booming. Because major vendors bundled C and C++ compilers, it was impossible to tell from sales data what the rate of C++ adoption or usage was. Since the products were generally referred to as C++ compilers, the assumption was that C++ was being heavily adopted.

Interestingly, analysts, the press, and customers were all telling us that the market needed templates and exception handling and that we'd better have them in our product. These relatively new C++ functions are for a variety of reasons hard to implement, so we knew we wouldn't be able to gratify this desire in the VC++ 1.0 time frame. And I suspected that the expressed need wasn't a real need. I kept asking myself, "Why do we need to put all of this complicated stuff into our product when I'll bet hardly anybody can use the stuff we've already got in the product? Why should we add more complicated stuff?" This was the beginning of a market theory. Pursue the anomalies in your information. That will often allow you to break free of the chains of conventional wisdom.

Pursue the anomalies in your information. That will often allow you to break free of the chains of conventional wisdom.

We did some research. It appeared that less than 15 percent of the market had moved from C to C++, although something like 80 percent planned to, wanted to, or hoped to in the next year or so. So we went around to talk to the customers. Customers often won't tell you what they really want, particularly if it goes against conventional wisdom. Because they're insecure, they'll tell you instead what they think they're supposed to say they want. That was the basic premise of our marketing theory: the customers were afraid of the technology, and developers were no different from applications users in that respect.

If you walk into a development shop and ask, "How many of you are incapable of learning C++?" people aren't going to raise their hands or jump to their feet and loudly proclaim, "Oh, me! I can't learn it! It's too hard!" No. They're going to say, "Well, we're waiting for templates and exceptions" or some such. You've got to dig a little deeper and touch on more profound needs than the purely technical ones.

The question to ask (preferably in private) is, "Are you having a hard time getting into this C++ thing?"

"Yeah. I don't have the time. It scares me. It's complicated. I really don't even know how to do Windows programming. I've read (or tried to read) a couple of books. I've watched the beginning of one video, which was lousy. But other people already know this stuff, and I'm falling behind. I'm afraid."

#17: *It's a relationship, not a sale.*

Find out what the customer needs. In the C++ business, at that moment, it became clear to us that our market couldn't get started with this complex new language. It was way too complicated. The customers just didn't know where to start. And Windows seemed impossible to program to anyway. They were still struggling with that. They really felt, You can't get a decent app up to save your life, with any amount of effort.

Conventional Wisdom

So some bright person in our group came up with a little device, a *wizard* thing. Now, it was just a little low-tech thing. It was not *really* a wizard. It was just a button that generates a bit of code. Conceptually, the wizard is one of the simplest things we ever did (although its underpinnings, MFC, were quite challenging). But the wizard hit the market sweet spot, enabling hundreds of thousands of C programmers to generate an application with the push of a button.

That wizard gave us dozens of points of market share growth. Low-tech is good. Help the customers. Find out what they want, what they're struggling with, and then turn *everything* in that direction. Forget templates, forget anything and everything except what the largest number of the potential customers truly want.

They want understanding. Gain that understanding of the customer, and then express that understanding in your product. Pivot your technology to do that. Tap into the customers' fantasies. In our case, the core customer fantasy went something like this: "I want to be a hotshot C++ programmer earning 90 thousand dollars a year. Now, if you can make that happen, and I don't have to learn anything, and I can then command that kind of money and the respect of my peers for being a C++ programmer, I'm going to buy your product! Nothing could keep me

"I'm going to buy your product! I will have a fight with my spouse in order to buy it. I will sacrifice almost anything to get it!"

from it. I will personally buy it if my company won't. I will have a fight with my spouse in order to buy it. I will sacrifice almost anything to get it!"

Think always of empowerment, security, control. Customers are not going to admit that they can't cope with your technology. A customer is not going to say, "Your software sucks." The customer is going to think, "I'm dumb." And the customers will stay away in droves until they think they've smartened up enough—or until your competitor makes them feel smart. You don't want to wait that long.

Your relationship with the customers is like a dance, or a love affair. You take steps (your releases and messages), and they take steps in response, and then you take more steps. You must be focused on the flow of transactions, on the overall pattern and direction, not on merely the latest transaction. This is all part of having that multi-release technology strategy I talked about in Rule #3. It's as good for your relationship with your customers as it is for your team. If your customers know (or sense) that you are going to be timely in your releases, that they are on a techno-chronological voyage with you, that you and they are going somewhere together, their expectations will smooth out over time.

But as in a love affair, should you neglect the beloved for too long, or otherwise signal your disinterest or rejection, the course of love won't run smooth. Your neglect will cause the market to feel betrayed, hurt, angry, and punitive. Don't be inconstant with your customers.

"I Must Be Dumb"

Recently I was on a plane, chatting with the woman in the next seat, and she asked me where I worked. Now, usually when you tell someone you work at Microsoft, you engender one of two responses. The person starts making superstitious gestures (throwing salt over her shoulder, blessing herself, forming her index fingers into a cross). Or the person immediately asks you if you know Bill Gates.

This woman took the latter tack, and after the Bill question, she began to talk about computers, describing her computer literacy plan to me. She was going to go to a community college, she said, and learn all about computers and software. She wanted to learn to operate a database, a spreadsheet, and a word processor. "Computers are wonderful," she said, "and I'm going to learn all about them—Windows, RAM, everything—even if it takes a couple of years."

I was of two minds as I listened to this woman and thought about her response to the personal computer revolution. I admired her courage, commitment, and foresight. She didn't want to be left behind, to miss out on one of the really big cultural shifts of our era. She was willing to invest large chunks of time, money, and effort to get acquainted with computers. Determined to face her lack of technical skill, she would address it head on.

"But wait a minute," I then thought to myself, "this woman has really bought in hard. Hook, line, and sinker hard. She is convinced that she ought to have to go back to school in order to learn to operate PC software. The software's not too hard. She's just too dumb! Yeah, you have to go to school, change yourself, learn all this gobbledy-gook to use my product. And then *you* give *me* money. Boy, this is a good gig, this making software. Even if I do a lousy job, and the thing is too difficult, the *customers* accept the blame. Using computers is *supposed* to be hard!"

If you're reading this book, you probably have a degree of computer proficiency, and your friends and family are probably aware of that. How many times has someone approached you, embarrassed and sheepish, and confessed that he or she knows "absolutely nothing" about computers? It's the same phenomenon. Most customers think something is wrong with them. It's almost a mass inferiority complex, an overwhelming insecurity: the world thinks the computer is right and they're wrong.

#18: *Cycle rapidly.*

Assuming you've learned how to ship a product at all, more or less with the quality and in the time frame you were after, it's good to start a program of cycling as rapidly as possible—for several reasons. First, no matter how fast you go, the market, or the technology, or the competition will be going faster. Possibly all three will be moving more quickly than you are. Second, your relationship with the market, like any relationship, is best maintained and enhanced with frequent and honest communication, and your primary communication with your market is carried in your product releases. Everything you have to say is in the product: your understanding, your passion, your purpose, your view of the customer, the qualities you believe in, who you are. Ain't no lies in the box. Your product embodies your identity.

I have never heard of a relationship—business or otherwise—that broke up because there was too much honest communication among the participants. By frequently updating your product, not only do you disclose yourself to the market, but by their purchase patterns and feedback the customers disclose themselves to you. Ain't no lies in cash money, either. It's in these transactions that your relationship with your customers lives; and the more frequent the transactions, the more dynamic the relationship.

In our Visual C++ group, we're cycling rapidly because now that we've figured out how to do it, we want to keep on doing it. This capability becomes a significant competitive weapon as well as the means to a dynamic market relationship. We've even gone so far as to market our product primarily as a subscription, delivered three times per year. I believe this avant-garde model for software delivery is a natural fit—but for two problems. Very few software outfits know how to ship with the regularity a subscription model mandates. And painless updates, without regression, are difficult to administer. As software development organizations grow capable of frequent shipment and the PC and network infrastructure matures, I expect this model to become commonplace.

From the customer's point of view, it's essential that he or she be able to pass on a given release. Customers might be preoccupied with internal releases of their own software, or with making other investments. Whatever the distraction, though, customers still don't want to be presented with a simple yes-or-no choice from you. Customers want to be able to plan their software absorption activities. To do this, they need to be able to predict the timing and probable impact of your next release. The current situation in software is largely one of major upgrades occurring randomly (in keeping with the immaturity of the development process) and alternating with hysterically planned and released bug fixes.

Shipping on time and shipping frequently pay bigger dividends than having great, major, revolutionary results infrequently. Be responsive instead of revolutionary. A subscription delivery model affords you the opportunity to do those "customer satisfaction only" releases to address just the things that drive your customers crazy. They'll be ecstatic if you do that. I find that fixing annoyances is often not a big deal, either. An annoyance fix is often low-tech, and usually the particular product behavior is so annoying that any progress at all comes as a relief to the customer.

I have found that customers prefer diskettes to promises—pretty much uniformly. There are some cases in which you need to give the customers a little bit of both promises and software, but in general the customers will love you if you give them new software. If you give them tap dancing, horns, and confetti, they may enjoy it but they won't give you any money.

A number of smaller efforts are almost always more desirable than a single larger one. A series of releases is infinitely more likely to yield the software your customers are craving. Shipping great software on time requires that we value small, understood solutions much more highly than big solutions fraught with unknowns.

The Design

Greatness in software is first of all a matter of getting the right product to the market at the right moment. That means you have to know how to ship and you have to discern the customers' deepest needs. The deeper the need it answers, the greater the software. The design of the software—"everybody participates in design"—is an expression of your team's total awareness and functionality. So the goal of any design process becomes incorporating the team's best ideas in a structure that when executing resolves the customer's deep needs.

Getting the best ideas expressed and available for analysis is the hardest part of the design process. But it is a supremely worthwhile effort. Think of it this way: With one or two people creating the design, you have 230 or maybe 250 IQ points migrating toward the box. With ten people, you might have as many as 1300 IQ points going into the box. Scale this exercise up with the size of your team. The point is that the more IQ you have generating and implementing design ideas, the greater the potential for great software. In every phase of design and implementation, there's substantial room for creativity. A single architect might have designed a great Gothic cathedral, but hundreds or even thousands of artisans each added value, realizing and individualizing the design.

Establishing a participatory environment that turns most team members on without slowing down the more gifted ones is a complex undertaking. This entire book is essentially devoted to that single challenge. And inculcating design values into the entire team is not the least challenging aspect of that tricky business. Teaching becomes the primary function of leaders and managers. Conduct workshops and case studies, *ad hoc,* when design problems arise. Make everything that happens a case in point.

#19: *Go for greatness.*

Surround the team with beauty, expect a high level of discourse, and seed personal growth by providing challenging reading and occasions for enriching voluntary assignments. Develop an esthetic in your group—centered on software design, of course, but drawn from the thousands of years of civilized human esthetic endeavor. The esthetic response is complicated and has been the subject of much thought throughout the centuries. Take advantage of all the work on the subject that has gone on before you. I'll plant a few ideas from that rich tradition here and there in this book just to get you started.

Shift the competitive playing field to the historical dimension. Think about the people and the achievements in history you find most admirable—recent history at first. Who and what accomplishments should inspire your own undertakings? How does the work your team is designing measure up? Will the work be seminal? Will it open up new veins of creative human potential? Will it be original in the sense that it will light the way to a new future no one had imagined before? Analyze the work's meaning in historical terms.

#20: *State your theme.*

Several surprisingly old texts on esthetics, ranging from George Santayana's 1896 classic, *The Sense of Beauty* (Scribners), to the more recent but hardly spanking-new work of George Stiny and James Gip in *Algorithmic Aesthetics* (University of California Press, 1978) have influenced my thinking about greatness in software. In the most recent of these texts, Stiny's and Gip's description of esthetics is right on the money in its application to the task we undertake when we talk about designing great software:

> Aesthetics is concerned with questions about how existing works of art can be described, interpreted, and evaluated, and with questions about how new works of art can be created.

I'm indebted to DeWitt H. Parker's *The Analysis of Art* (Yale University Press, 1926) for the criteria I ask the team to bring to their analysis of a software design. From Parker I get six criteria (Parker says "the six elements") of esthetic form.

According to Parker, *unity* is the master principle of great art. And I have seen over and over that unity is the master principle of great software. If we adapted Parker's explanation of unity, we'd say that in a product that had unity, each element would be essential to the value of the whole and all essential elements would be there. From Parker, too, come the corollaries that since everything the customer needed would be there, the customer wouldn't be tempted to go beyond the present experience, and that since nothing would be there that wasn't required, the customer's absorption into the world of the product wouldn't be disturbed. Unity of purpose as well as unity in the executing program should be the hallmark of your team's effort. You achieve unity in a work of art, according to Parker, by observing the following creative principles, whether you arrive at the principles intuitively or rationally. I've adapted Parker's principles in the interest of achieving unity in software.

The *theme* of your software is the dominant idea that constitutes the basis of the design. All of the values of the product must stem from the theme. And if the developers and the market are to comprehend the theme, you must render it with surpassing clarity. Theme is equivalent to *purpose*. The more specific the purpose of the product, the greater its impact. Having a theme for the product means that you eliminate or at least minimize orthogonal values. This reduction can be a painful process, and, yes, it involves risk. But once you decide what the theme is, you have to sacrifice other qualities, qualities that don't support the theme—even if they're qualities you cherish that are expressive of your fondest and longest-held beliefs.

Messages flow from themes. An astute observer simply examining the product will articulate the message if the theme stands out. Having a good message that's only partially supported by the product's theme won't do. Neither will having a good message that's backed by mixed themes. Your theme stems from your market theory. In our Visual C++ 1.0 case, our market theory was that people were having a hard time getting started with C++. The theme of our design was, "Make it easier to get started with C++." The message, of course, echoed that theme: "Visual C++ 1.0 makes it easy to get started with C++." Duh.

The point is that your product shouldn't be just a grab bag of features. Chop off (almost) everything that doesn't support the theme. You've got to have a purpose for your product, and "unity of purpose" is a good phrase to describe the impact of having a theme. Then put the money behind the purpose, and get everybody on the team aware of the purpose and contributing to it. If you'll do that, you'll ship a product that embodies the purpose.

Getting Single-Minded

I don't know whether or not this story is apocryphal, but I like it anyway. A spreadsheet development team did some studies that led them to the conclusion that people most often used their product to type in 20 numbers or so and then wanted to be able to generate a chart from the numbers. The team discovered that this was the majority case.

So they worked on that and worked on that and worked on that until that one capability, being able to type in a few numbers and then produce a chart, was simple and easy. Customers who used the spreadsheet program to produce charts were very happy. In their eyes, that one capability justified the purchase.

A similar story—I don't know whether this one's true, either—has to do with one of the home financial packages. The team on this project evaluated the market and said, "The purpose of our product is quick gratification, or we'll lose them, and they'll never buy an upgrade." They decided that they wanted an arbitrary beginner to be able to load and run their program and within ten minutes be getting productive results. They'd fine-tune over several releases if they had to, to get that time down to ten minutes.

(continued)

Getting Single-Minded *continued*

So they all went out to various computer stores and followed the people who bought their product home—presumably, they asked permission. Then they watched carefully, noting, for example, even how the product was unwrapped and what the customer looked at first, what troubles the customer ran into during setup and the initial program run, and so on. And they saw dozens of opportunities to intensify the customer's gratification, and they seized on those opportunities voraciously. And through a period of several releases, they achieved their goal of ten-minute gratification.

Variation is the product's theme restated and elaborated in slightly altered and embroidered ways. Variation is the means by which we intensify the user's comprehension and appreciation of our theme while we continue to pique interest and leverage the user's growing consciousness in new ways.

Evolution in a product means that earlier parts determine later parts. Lessons learned in earlier, simpler, parts of the product apply to later, more complex, parts. Things thus progress in a way that is pleasing. Outcomes, if not predictable, are satisfying because the product foreshadows them in countless ways.

Balance in a product is the allocation of appropriate emphasis among the various elements of the product. Opposing or contrasting elements, for instance, have equal weight.

Hierarchy is having the elements of the product gain attention in proportion to their importance. Closely related to the property of balance, hierarchy provides a means for establishing and evaluating balance. If the theme is the top of the hierarchy, elements at the next level should have balanced value with respect to each other, all equally supporting the thematic function, and so on throughout the rest of the hierarchy.

Beautiful Properties

In 1975, Guy Sircello developed an interesting line of esthetic reasoning in *A New Theory of Beauty* (Princeton University Press). I won't go into the clever distinction Sircello made between qualitative and quantitative properties of objects, but Sircello did reason to my satisfaction that what we perceive as beauty in an object is really beauty in one or more of the object's qualitative properties. Sircello reasoned further that a property is beautiful only if it is present in the object to a high degree and that an object is beautiful only if it contains at least one of these plentifully present properties. A sufficiency of a beautiful property is not necessarily enough to make an object beautiful, but an object can't be beautiful without at least one such intensely realized property.

Does Sircello's theory shed some light on the failure of products that contain everything but the kitchen sink, on products that try to "do it all"? In such products, the idea of one or two intensely realized properties gives way to the accumulation of a large number of properties, a long list of features, so that no property is sufficiently intense to get the product out of the "insipid" category.

#21: *Minimize dependencies.*

A dependency is any necessary thing not under the team's control. The fewer dependencies allowed into the project at the beginning, the better off everyone and the project will be. It's a fact of life that the general level of software development proficiency is low. Even if you do your part well and with regard for timeliness, the other guy may very well not.

Design time is when dependencies get bound into the project. The team should be conscious of the tremendous potential cost of dependencies. Make allowing any dependency into the project a very serious matter. Subject each prospective dependency to the intensest scrutiny by everyone, and research the likelihood of the other guy's or the other team's coming through for you.

#22: *Propitiate the gods.*

A golfer throws a ball into the lake before teeing off to satisfy the water-hazard gods. Some of your dependencies and your other unknowns are bound to get you. Pick the one or the few that are most likely to get you, and take whatever steps you have to to excise them from your project.

How do you choose such features? Pick the dependency or the iffy feature that means the least to you in terms of ultimate customer satisfaction. Yes, the customer might be peeved at you for not including the feature in the current release, but since you ship frequently and on time (!), the customer won't abandon you. The customer will wait instead to see whether you pick up the desired feature appropriately in the next release.

Appease the Gods

#23: *Portability is for canoes.* _____

The complexity of multi-platform support is beyond the reach of most software development organizations. Even discounting the added development burden, with the addition of each platform, the job of QA increases exponentially. Clever QA management can minimize the burden somewhat, but you'll do better to regulate your bets. Demand multi-platform support from your system software vendor, and then build your product on the absolute fewest number of platforms possible.

And choose carefully. Picking the wrong platform(s) can be fatal.

#24: *Design time at design time.* _____

Put time into your design. Don't create a design and then try to determine how long it will take to implement. Time is one of the primary media with which you are working.

The product will ship when the design can be shown to be implemented. Developers and their managers often ignore the exigencies of time when they create a design. Instead, you should consider the implementation time as a critical design element. When you evaluate design alternatives, disadvantage the one that takes longer to implement. Often, when you give appropriate design value to timeliness, you can substantially compress implementation time.

A product that is not designed to ship on time…won't. One that is…probably won't. The latter is preferable to the former. Duh.

Development

By "development," I mean the actual activities—planning, scheduling, creating, and validating the software product—regardless of which people in which software development discipline perform which function. Everybody on the team is engaged in the process of software development. Hence, everybody is a developer.

It's interesting to note that the predominant word in common parlance for the activity of software creation is "development." The idea of "development," of course, implies some kind of maturation process, a moving through a sequence of interdependent steps. What's doing the moving in software development? It's the team ideation, gradually migrating from highly individual (even private) notions toward a group articulation in the shipping code. This line of reasoning brings us full circle (again!) to one of my favorite themes: the development of individual ideas into intellectual property is the essential act of software development.

The end of software development is software developers.

Software Session

But the development goes on in several dimensions. Each individual is developing, the team dynamics are developing, the underlying technology is developing. Software development is development without apparent beginning or end, affecting all who enter into its many dimensions. Yes, there are these events properly called "releases" that do express the state of all this ongoing development. But let's not mistake an individual release for the end product of this unrelenting multi-level development process. The end of software development is software developers.

Many experts have analyzed the process of software development in engineering terms, and it is often thought of as an engineering problem. I see software development as primarily a sociological or cultural phenomenon. Working with the individual developers and the team that evolves to create clarity of purpose is far more difficult and infinitely more essential than a particular design methodology or the particulars of the engineering fundamentals. Software engineering prowess is necessary, but prowess alone is not sufficient.

During the opening moves, "development" involves the solution of many simultaneous equations. The equations have mainly to do with the vagaries of scheduling and the increasing illumination of the feature content. Remember that in the beginning it's not usual to know precisely what's going to be in the product when all is said and done. At this point, features are known by their names (sometimes) and their general expected functionality, but the design is usually incomplete and will remain so until the release is made. That means that one especially complex equation involves factoring out huge amounts of uncertainty with respect to rapidly evolving features while imaginatively projecting their destination.

Software development is more like a jam session than an orchestrated event.

Another labyrinthine equation that must be devised in the opening moves is an equation to account for the infinite variability in the effectiveness and creativity of the individual contributors. Not only must we fully imagine the feature content, but we must predict how and when it will evolve and become congealed in working bits at the hands of individual inventors.

This complexity makes scheduling a somewhat ludicrous undertaking. Naturally, you'll establish an overall goal for the product's completion, and you'll focus the team's efforts on meeting the first milestone, a couple of months out from the project's beginnings, but that's about the most you can hope to accomplish in the opening moves. (We will go into milestones in some detail later, when we take up the middle game, but the important thing to realize about milestones both now and later is that they give you the opportunity to "practice shipping" at regular intervals, intervals not greater than a few months apart.)

Software development is more like a jam session than an orchestrated event. When you're jamming, the important thing is to know when to come in, when to go to the forefront, when to recede, how to syncopate with the other players to create rhythms, and how to climax in a flurry of group improvisation. The jam might sound as if it were orchestrated and planned to the last triplet, but it's actually as spontaneous as joy itself.

#25: *Don't accept dictation.*

I am amazed at the extent to which the software development community accepts bogus dictates, especially when it comes to scheduling. This astonishing passivity is emblematic of Old World behavior applied to New World problems. Given that it's extremely difficult (probably impossible) for a team of committed professionals to create a schedule that even approximates the rate at which the product ultimately materializes, it's utter madness that in many organizations the dates, the features, and the resources—the holy triangle—of a software development project are dictated by people unfamiliar with developing software. Too often people like "Upper Management" or "Marketing" or some other bogeymen conjure up the date. What's worse, by some malignant and pervasive twist of illogic, otherwise competent development managers accept this sort of folly as standard operating procedure.

I have polled dozens of groups of development managers, and my informal data gathering suggests that somewhere in the neighborhood of 30 to 40 percent of all development efforts suffer from dictated features, resources, and schedules.

The ultimate act of disempowerment is to take away the responsibility for the schedule from those who must live by it.

It should be a fundamental dogma that the person who has to do the work should predict the amount of time it will take. Of course, if accuracy isn't a goal, anybody can make the foolish predictions.

In some ways, the root of all scheduling evil is that software developers and their managers abdicate their responsibility to determine the probable effort required to achieve a given set of results. The ultimate act of disempowerment is to take away the responsibility for the schedule from those who must live by it. To accept this treatment under any circumstances is no less heinous an act than imposing a bogus scheduling imperative on a team to begin with.

It's easy to sympathize with the urge for control and predictability that this phenomenon manifests, but why on earth should such organizational goofiness persist in the face of what always follows, repeated software calamity?

Often people and organizations have a hard time learning from their mistakes. We tend to be a bit thick sometimes. Our diagnosis of what went wrong the last time can be utterly erroneous, and so we gear up to do it all again—without ever even beginning to experience the core insights required for successful software development.

This blindness is especially likely after a disastrously late software project. Many team members desperately want never to repeat such a death march, so they leave the group. As evidenced by their urge to survive, these people are often the most vital members of the team. The remnant is left lurching about in a fog of blame. Like the Angel of Death, Guilt visits every cubicle. The managers are choking on their own failure, so their ability to lead is smothered. The marketing people have been made to look foolish, their promises just so much gas, and cynicism creeps into their messages. The executives are bewildered, embarrassed, and angry. The customers have been betrayed yet another time.

Keep in mind that in an asylum, the sane are crazy.

Slowly the fog dissipates, and a modicum of hope materializes. New team members re-inject a measure of the lost vitality into the team, and new (or forgetful) managers take the helm. The technological siren seduces the group once again. The executives, chastened but unlearning, plunk down more dough and tell the team when the new project must be done. The cycle repeats.

How is a person to cope with such folly? If you find yourself in such an organizational situation, how should you respond? Keep in mind that in an asylum, the sane are crazy. And in an organization in which irrationality prevails, the irrationality tends to concentrate the further up you go. Your situation might be hopeless because the extent to which you are viewed as crazy will tend to intensify in direct proportion to the power of the observer. You might be able to cope with irrational and self-destructive organizational values, but you're unlikely to prosper in such a setting.

A situation this gravely out of whack must be resolved, however. So you steel yourself and inform your dictators that, much as you would like to accept their dictates, you are unable to do so because reality requires otherwise. You remind them (tactfully) that their power is not magic, that their wishes don't make software. You help them envision a future in which people are striving to meet *their own* goals, things they've proposed to do over a certain interval and things that have a chance of being done even sooner than anticipated.

You need to build schedules meticulously from the bottom up. Each person who has a task to do must own the design and the execution of that task and must be held accountable for its timely achievement. Accountability is the twin of empowerment. The two together can create a reasonable software development plan.

#26: *Now go play.*

Viewed as work, software development is a pretty unattractive profession. Find another view of it. I suggest you see it as play.

If you buy my theory that the team and the software are equivalent, you'll expect the team with more spontaneity, quicker reflexes, more humor, and more

Guilt Visits a Cubicle

lightness of touch to produce the most pleasurable and least annoying software. You can win the game only by *playing* the game. Computers are the ultimate toy, and developers, the ultimate gamesters.

The opening moves are not the things you do first in a sequence of steps that lead ultimately to software success.

In a healthy team, play will tend to occur naturally. Managers don't need to take special steps. All you have to do is avoid constraining human nature and look for signs of joy and spontaneity. Fan the embers of happiness and bliss. And don't confuse play with distraction. The distracted team is all business.

The game of software rewards and punishes those who play it well and foolishly according to its own nature and principles of play. Don't worry about dispensing justice and arbitration. The game itself sorts things out many times more efficiently and intensely than you can.

How do you get good at the game? Play it, practice it, enjoy it, and love it. Effectiveness in software creation will drive out rigidity and supercilious seriousness of purpose. Let it happen.

The opening moves are not the things you do first in a sequence of steps that lead ultimately to software success. Rather, they are the preparations you must make within yourself and together with the team before you can achieve your highest potential. These preparations are not a "program" for success. They're a prerequisite of greatness. If the things we've considered in this "Opening Moves" part of the book are happening at all, they're happening simultaneously and repetitively as your development team develops.

The Middle Game

Although it's difficult to divide the software development process into discrete stages, it is a worthwhile effort to categorize the overlapping stages of the process in some way. We need some schema to help us organize and focus our efforts serially. I haven't put the topics I cover in each section into an arbitrary chronology, but neither should you take away the impression that the only time to think about or act on a particular issue is during the stage of the game to which I've assigned its discussion. Virtually all of the analysis and the rules of thumb in this book are things you should be aware of continuously and repetitively. As your expertise develops, your ability to simultaneously prioritize, reconcile, and apply all of these techniques will become more or less continuous.

If the opening moves are concerned primarily with envisioning a team and a product, the middle game is about expectations, uncertainty, and struggle. In the middle game, where nothing is clear and the terror of failure is pervasive, perseverance becomes the goal. Regardless of the team's maturity, the number of times you've all been through it, or the ultimate greatness of the product you're creating, the middle game is always frightening and disorienting, full of nasty surprises and unexpected failures. Count on it.

In every project, there comes a time when you wish with all your heart that there were some way out. Everything is in doubt. Cynicism and mutiny are in the air. No one has seen land for months. The crew is suffering from scurvy, the larder is empty, the stormy seas seem endless.

Welcome to the middle game.

#27: *Be like the doctors.*

Doctors mostly manage to retain a modicum of respect and social approbation without pandering to the fears and insecurities of their patients, all of whom are

The Middle Game

destined to die. Theirs is a good model for setting expectations. Software development, like medicine, is not an exact science. It's unfortunate that software development isn't yet generally recognized as an art form that happens to have technical aspects.

For now, we really have to learn to be like the doctors. They are able to say, quite comfortably and confidently and with conviction, "These things are never certain." Doctors seldom if ever state with certainty what the outcome of any procedure might be. Yet software managers, operating in a far less disciplined and less data-driven environment, one with much less history and of a complexity perhaps equal to the complexity of the anatomical systems that are the doctor's purview, blithely promise features, dates, and outcomes not especially susceptible to prediction. Worse, doctors are usually dealing with a subsystem that is malfunctioning while the overall system remains largely functional. In software development, the goal is often a wholly new system that has never functioned before at all.

"Of course, there's always some risk in even simple procedures…"

Another good expectation-setting line that software developers should borrow from the doctors is, "Of course, there's always some risk in even simple procedures…" If that hedge doesn't express the essential hazard of even the least tweak to a program, I don't know what does.

The thing to keep in mind is that there is at least one good model for dealing with uncertainty with some degree of integrity. It's best for the patient to know (insofar as they're knowable) the risks and uncertainties he or she faces. It's best for those involved in or dependent upon a software development process to know about the risks and the uncertainties, too.

#28: *Remember the triangle: Features, Resources, Time.* _____

As a development manager, you're working with only three things: resources (people and money), features (the product and its quality), and the schedule. This triangle of elements is all you work with. There's nothing else to be worked with. And changing one side of the triangle has an impact on at least one other side, usually two. So if the project starts to slip (time), go back to the triangle and examine the impact on resources and features. Or whenever somebody discusses features, you can seem to be very smart if you immediately start to discuss schedule, or resources. It's a simple enough matter to mentally run through the sides of the triangle, or to force others to, anytime one side of the triangle comes up. "OK, I have to work on one of these legs of the triangle in order to recover from this slip, or maybe on all three legs. I add a little resource, I trim a few features, and I move the schedule out a bit." Since the people, the product, or the schedule is almost always what you're discussing, constantly envision the triangle. You'll find that this leads to the most fruitful lines of thought.

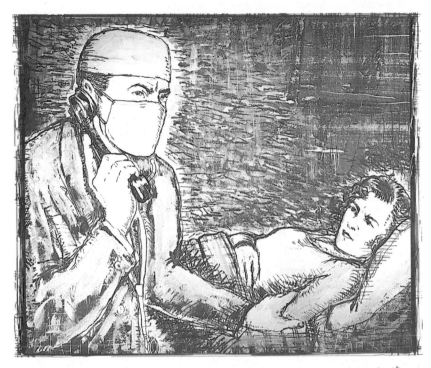

"These Things Are Never Certain"

When considering the possible solutions to a schedule shortfall, keep in mind that there are only four possible: add time, subtract features, add resources, or do some combination of the three.

"Don't Throw More People at a Problem"?

How many times have you heard that throwing people at a schedule shortfall is a bad idea? Fred Brooks, in his classic book on software development *The Mythical Man-Month,* went to great lengths to make the point that adding people to a software development project inappropriately could actually slow down the effort. This is a very wise insight, but the key word is "inappropriately." Brooks's lesson has been too successful in some ways. We should keep in mind that he wrote a book, not a single one-size-fits-all epigram.

(continued)

Remember the Triangle

Conventional wisdom, ever the oversimplifier, has reduced Brooks's genuine wisdom to the simple axiom, "Never add people to an ongoing development project." Nine times out of ten, that's probably appropriate advice, but too many development managers now avoid *ever* adding people to a project. They feel paralyzed in this regard. Adding people is an extremely difficult step to manage, and it's generally not the first solution to a schedule shortfall you should consider, but it is one of the alternatives you can consider.

#29: *Don't know what you don't know.*

It is essential not to profess to know, or to seem to know, or to accept that someone else knows, that which is unknown. Almost without exception, the things that end up coming back to haunt you are the things you pretended to understand early on but didn't. At virtually every stage of even the most successful software projects, there are large numbers of very important things that are unknown. It is acceptable—even mandatory—to articulate your ignorance, so that no one misjudges the state of things, how much is still unknown. If you don't cultivate and disseminate a "lucid ignorance," disaster will surely befall you.

Human nature is such that we dislike not knowing things that are important to our well-being. Since there is so much that we don't know in a software project, the nearly universal tendency among developers and their managers is to gloss over or even deny altogether the extent of their ignorance. Treasure and reward team members who consistently make themselves aware of the list of relevant things that are currently unknown. Resisting the natural human cravings for certainty and order calls for moral and psychological strength. It's especially difficult to acknowledge uncertainty when the true state of affairs is covered over by a veneer of orderliness, which is often the case. Pseudo-order is one maladaptive defense against uncertainty.

Pseudo-order is one maladaptive defense against uncertainty.

I'm suggesting that a great deal of your effort should go into making sure that all the people on the project are aware of their ignorance rather than naively converting it to falsehoods. Bear down on the team until they realize that they haven't comprehensively assessed the unknowns. In the successful project, this is much easier in the early stages, or during times of change. This is no time to mince words. People ultimately prefer success even if discomfort and disillusionment are prerequisites.

Lucid Ignorance

The organization around you will recoil from the uncertainty you insist they face, clinging to pseudo-order and making countless attempts to magically convert ignorance to knowledge. Your job is to make uncertainty an unshakable fact, and then to coerce the reshaping of the organization to cope with the uncertain situation. For its own well-being, the organization must learn to thrive in an uncertain environment.

Now that I've put it into a book, let's say it's official: when something is unknown, the best policy is to state that simple fact, even if the unknown is not knowing when the software will ship. Don't worry about it. No one can be hired to take your place who will be able to know the unknown.

Needless to say, the people who work with me get more points for not knowing something, and for knowing that they don't know it, than they do for knowing something. I'd rather know what the unknowns are. I want to know what's going to get me. The people I work for would rather know that, too.

The goal on a software development project is not to have the correct plan in advance but to make the right decisions every day as things that were unknown become known. If you've been pretending that you know something you don't, you won't be able to take advantage of the true information when it becomes known. You'll also be left in the uncomfortable position of having been proven wrong by emergent information. This will tend to put you in opposition to finding out more because of its immense personal cost. And when you set yourself up in a posture in which you seem to be resisting knowledge, your stock invariably declines.

The only uncertainties that get resolved are the ones that have been identified as such. Unidentified uncertainties simply bite you. That's considerably more uncomfortable than an awareness of uncertainty is.

When you don't understand how something's going to be accomplished, when a quiet inner voice whispers barely perceptible doubts to you, go with it. Don't be afraid to seem dumb by admitting that you don't know something and asking for an explanation from the people you assume do know. You'll either learn something or learn something else. Often that quiet voice inside you is tuning into the group's unconscious doubts, and you are just the receiver. So many times people will respond to your question with, "Yeah, I was wondering the same thing!" Of course, occasionally your question will make everybody think you're clueless. That's simply the price you pay from time to time for exposing uncertainty. (If your hit rate is really low, you may need to take remedial steps.)

Integrity

Integrity is about balance and congruence. Do words and deeds balance? Or thoughts and words? Intent and practice? When we speak together, do we say what is on our minds? Do we let people drive us in ways we don't want to go? Is our behavior incongruous with our feelings or desires? When we commit to a direction, do we stay the course? Do we really agree, or are we only giving the impression we agree?

Integrity is about honesty and hypocrisy. When I do something, am I doing it because of its inherent value or only because it appears to others to have value? Am I more interested in protecting appearances than in honest progress? Am I willing to act as if I think something is a good idea when I don't? Do I really believe what I allow people to assume I believe?

Integrity is about truth. The only thing harder than telling the truth is knowing the truth. When all around me are confirming one another's fantasies and magically converting wishes to reality; when I have only the vaguest sensation that something is not quite right; when conventional wisdom and group think are strangling a new, emergent reality being born in me, can I know, and tell, my truth?

#30: Don't go dark.

You approach a milestone date and ask the lead developer, "How's it going? Are we going to hit the milestone?"

"Well," she answers, "I've been doing really well for the last six weeks, but today, you know, things were really bad and I slipped six months."

No. Slips happen a little bit at a time. Slips don't happen at the end of the milestone or the project. Slips just show up at the end. But they happen every day. They happen every hour. Every time someone has to make a fresh pot of coffee, answer unexpected e-mail, reconfigure a machine, or track down a maddeningly intermittent but catastrophic bug, slips happen.

You have to manage the granularity of development tasks in such a way that you emerge with visible deliverables over short intervals. In our group, we argue back and forth over how big the intervals should be: five days, ten days, three weeks? In our world, three weeks is going dark.

I don't know what's appropriate for your world, but we want team members to have contracts with the other parts of the team so that they surface pretty often

Don't Go Dark

with visible components. When somebody surfaces and the deliverable isn't done, we know right away. We know that this week we slipped one day. That's worth knowing, much better than getting to the end of the project and observing, "Oh, we slipped six months!" At that point, it's too late to even bother counting up how much you've slipped. That's the world's worst experience.

On second thought, the world's worst experience—or one almost as bad—is the sense that you're lost in a software development project. (See the box.) Often in the middle game you experience a profound sense of confusion. You feel, "I don't know what to do. I don't know if we're close or far away. All I know is that I don't feel very good. And that any change I make is going to screw up everything else, I'm pretty sure. But then everything is already screwed up, so maybe . . ." That terrible sequence of thoughts (the software manager's fugue state) comes from going dark, walking around with the lights off. Turn the lights on. Get the team to buy into a granular approach.

Lost in Software

I won't waste time establishing that the lateness of software is a huge and pervasive problem. If it weren't, you probably wouldn't be reading this book. Just ask any assembled group of software developers or managers if they have ever been seriously late on a software project, or even if they are usually late on a software project. There are only two likely answers to such a question: yes or a falsehood of some sort. The falsehood may be incredibly buffered schedules that render the concept of timeliness absurd, or it may be significantly under-featured software.

An even scarier question to ask the group of software developers and managers is, "How many of you have been *lost* on a software development project?"

They'll usually know exactly what you mean. Being lost in software is terrifying. Dozens of theories about what's wrong with the project circulate, each negating the other, all tending to promote overall paralysis. A sense of doom infects the team members. Order breaks down. Wild schemes are proposed in all seriousness. Dread, panic, despair, and a mad sort of hopefulness break out at random. You don't really know what's happening—you can't identify the problem—and you simply don't know what to do. Any action you contemplate makes huge negative consequences loom in your mind. You have no freedom to act.

You're thrown on your instincts at a time when your confidence is shattered. After all, if your instincts were so great, how in the hell did you get into this mess? Plus, everybody smells your fear, and they have lost faith in your instincts, too. You can work no magic amidst the unbelievers.

Most software development managers will relate to these feelings.

Now, of course, as soon as you tell the team, "I want your deliverables every week," they'll say, "You're micro-managing me!" You make that acceptable by having other people depend on them, people who need those deliverables. The QA guys need a deliverable. The documentation people need a deliverable.

Lost in Software

The developers need the test results the day after they pass out their deliverable. The team interdependencies become the motivation, not some heavy-handed management dictum.

Some features will have long development lead times—months or even years—but slips will usually happen a little bit every day and must be compensated for a little bit every day. This calls for a granularity of development tasks such that deliverables are achieved at intervals sufficiently small that slips can be compensated for. A week is a long time to go without knowing what is happening. Yes, micro-management is always a danger, and that accusation will certainly be leveled against you from time to time, but if the goal of the project is to ship great software on time, and if everybody makes that goal uppermost, they'll usually enjoy the chase. And team interdependencies are a powerful motivational force, too.

The goal is to create a network of self-motivated individual commitments. Just as the goal of software design is to get all of the best ideas of the team into the box, the goal of managing deliverables (or, as we call them, handshakes) is to get each of the team's individual promises into the box. Mary Developer commits to Joe Documenter that her feature will be ready for explanation by Friday. Now Mary's credibility with Joe is involved in the project. Their relationship is one component of the development process. If, on the other hand, Bill Manager tells Howard Developer that his component *must* be complete by Friday, all of Howard Developer's authority complexes become a part of the development process, not to mention Bill's insecure authority facade. These dynamics can be exciting and psychologically engaging, but they seldom produce the results you're after. Ah, the joys and perils of intellectual property creation! There's simply no escaping the complexities of the human psyche when that psyche is the direct source of the product.

Earlier I mentioned that what is being developed is not clear. To avoid going entirely dark, we need to see that the real development task is to create a community capable of making and keeping hundreds of small but vital promises. This has little to do with technology *per se* and much to do with integrity in the face of uncertainty.

#31: *Beware of a guy in a room.*

This is really a special case of "Don't go dark" that's worth calling out separately.

Once upon a time (actually three times upon a time, but I'm too embarrassed to recite all three cases), the best developer in our group was given the hardest assignment on a particular project. Wilhelm. Everybody agreed that Wilhelm was the best. He was the most experienced, imaginative, technically accomplished, and gifted developer on the team. Nobody questioned his talent or his judgment.

Beware of a Man in a Room

When it was time for Wilhelm to begin his work on this most challenging feature, off he went into his office with the aquarium, the eclectic music collection (heavy metal and Mozart), his inflated rubber Gumby, and his *Star Trek* posters.

Beads of sweat appeared on his forehead. His stress was palpable.

With a six-pack of Mountain Dew and a generous supply of No-Doz, he shut himself up. The rest of us were brimming with confidence, having so wisely delegated this important task to Wilhelm, great development figure that he was. We would listen to his keys clickety-clack hour upon hour, day after day, as he programmed with a fury from behind his shut door. We would smile securely, knowing that the fate of our entire company was in the stubby but effective hands of the indefatigable Wilhelm.

(And isn't it ever thus—when our vision seems most clear, our security most deep, and our cleverness most beguiling; when for a moment we relax in a confident stupor or for an instant we have the conviction that we are executing a well-designed plan—do not then the remorseless and vengeful software specters arise, wail, and strike?)

Gradually, it became clear to us that Wilhelm was having difficulty. He never went home now. His fish went unfed. The music had stopped. Beads of sweat appeared on his forehead. His stress was palpable, his Gumby deflated. Wilhelm was…late.

Wilhelm had no deliverables but the completed feature. Everybody else was done. We knocked on his door. "Wilhelm," we shouted through the door, "how's it goin'?" knowing full well that our struggle was just beginning.

"Pretty good," he responded tardily.

"When will you be done?" we asked.

There was a long pause. You could almost hear the tears welling in his eyes. "Soon," he said disconsolately.

We knew that "soon" meant "not soon." Now the entire company came to a standstill. No one did anything but wait for Wilhelm. I, the manager, the accountable one, faced difficult choices. I could fire Wilhelm. The fact that he's the only one in the universe who can get me out of this trap, the only one who understands the problem he's facing, I rashly reasoned, shouldn't keep me from removing Wilhelm

"For my part, I must simply buy large quantities of Mountain Dew."

from the scene. We'll just start over! No, that was obviously out of the question. Wilhelm was, after all, our best developer and the only developer who knew the problem inside and out.

A better solution, I thought next, would be to pressure Wilhelm, to make sure that he's doubly aware that the fate of all his colleagues, their children, and their children's children is riding upon the efficiency of his stubby fingers and his unusual mentality. Yes, hound him by the hour, have people take shifts, redoubling his stress again and again, unremittingly.

But no, that seemed on second thought to be counterproductive, too. There was no way out of the trap. None. I was left with, "Wilhelm will finish if he doesn't die or quit. And he will never do anything for me again. For my part, I must simply buy large quantities of Mountain Dew."

Of course, if you have a guy in a room you might have a pathological situation, or you might have a healthy pattern of creative behavior. One pathology is a kind of savior complex that can't be satisfied unless the developer blows every single deadline but the last and then emerges victoriously with a brilliant piece of work five minutes late. A more healthy pattern is that of the true innovator who is designing something great but who has no personal resources left over for anything but the work at hand. The work consumes every ounce of psychological, emotional, and intellectual energy. Teamwork is an insignificant concern to a person immersed in this sort of creative experience.

Specialist developers who lock themselves away in a room, who go dark for long stretches, are anathema to shipping great software on time. No matter how brilliant a developer might be, don't give the developer a significant assignment unless he or she understands and buys into the type of development program you intend to run. The brilliant developer must be capable of performing on a team, making his work visible in modest increments and subjecting it to scrutiny as it matures. Some people find this intolerable, and although there is a role for people of this disposition in the software world, it is not as part of a team devoted to shipping great software on time.

Regardless of whether the cause is bogus or healthy, the results of allowing a guy to stay in a room are uniformly fatal to the professional development organization. Beware. Extricating your project from this trap is nearly impossible.

#32: *If you build it, it will ship.*

If you build it, it will ship. If you don't, it won't. Seems pretty obvious, doesn't it? But I don't mean "build it once and ship it." I mean "build it often and regularly." You must get that product visible. Public.

Can you imagine blindfolding dozens or even hundreds of people and turning them loose to construct a building without seeing what they were doing? It's essential to build the software product under construction as frequently as possible. The point of this rule is to engage the team in building the product *frequently, regularly, throughout the development cycle,* with *the highest possible quality,* and in a *public place* where all team members can have access to it.

The product should be built, if not every day, then at frequent intervals, along with all setup scripts and online help, in a public place, where QA can conduct

Surface the Product

appropriate assessment of daily status and the entire team can observe progress or its lack. The regular build is the single most reliable indicator that a team is functional and a product is being developed.

Your build strategy is worth substantial thought and investment. Many groups at Microsoft have focused on creating a daily build of their product, with a "build master" and a build group to support the process. Elaborate procedures ensure that the build never breaks. Multiple sign-offs before code check-ins are routinized, build breakage results in public humiliation for the offenders, and individual accountability for the smoothness of the daily build is taken to extremes. You could do worse than institute a policy such as this one, since a rigorous daily build is probably the most effective way to get to a known state and stay there. (See the next rule.)

On the other hand, you are after the optimum procedure for your group, not absoluteness. Even if you don't build every day, the point of this rule is to get you to put effort into your build activities and to improve the timeliness of your builds—at the very least.

Personally, I'm not sure what the optimal investment in building a product in its entirety should be, but I am convinced that it's a larger investment than most development organizations currently make! Every day might be too often, although I've seen that relentless build schedule work and work well, but it is clear to me that every week is beginning to push the outer limits of acceptability for projects of almost any size.

The product must be made visible. You have to see what you are doing. Even if you've created a network of individual commitments and short-term deliverables and you've carefully avoided going dark in the development plan, all is for naught if you don't build the system. You are going dark *de facto*. And all sense of reality will derive from imaginings informed more by people's psychological history than by the reality of current events.

Every day you can count the bugs, and you can count the progress, and you can see the emerging functionality.

In order to be visible, the product must be buildable. In order to maintain buildability, you have to uphold a certain level of quality. The introduction of egregious errors becomes immediately apparent, and big steps backward become intolerable. Maintaining a frequent build discipline instills a certain orderliness and quality consciousness in the team.

More important, perhaps, a daily build (or a build at some other frequent, regular interval) creates a heartbeat for the team. Every day, at four o'clock, say, the entire system is built. Everybody can see the result of all of the day's efforts at five o'clock. It's visible. Progress attends the daily build ritual. If the daily build fails, or doesn't happen for some reason, the "heartbeat monitors" start to screech insistently, demanding emergency attention. A chronically failing build is the surest symptom of a failing (or seriously struggling) project. And a build schedule methodically "thumping along" is a great source of reassurance.

Don't confuse this build process with autonomous developer-driven builds conducted on an individual's machine. I'm talking about a public build of the official source tree that everybody and anybody can look at and play with, on which QA can run what we call "sniff tests" that validate the basic functionality of the system, preemptively catching gross regressions. By building the product every day, by having a build person who is accountable for the build, you greatly increase your odds of never losing functionality. Everybody can see that the product is getting closer and closer and closer to your goal. Every day you can count the bugs, and you can count the progress, and you can see the emerging functionality. And then everybody can play with the same product, and all can know where they're at based on the same information.

There are numerous other critical advantages to the policy of building the product consistently:

❖ A frequent, public build exposes the real (vs. the imagined) dependency tree. The product just plain won't build if everything isn't properly lined up. Getting through the build is like working through the dependencies, both the internal ones and those external to the development organization. *Everybody* can see what's causing the hangups.

❖ The build exposes unanticipated weaknesses in the design, things that are too often left until too late in the development cycle for appropriate remediation, things like performance or size problems.

❖ The build is the natural mechanism to get everybody working on the same thing at the same time. One constant problem in software development is the coordination of versions. The worst case is one version per person. For a build, everybody has to synchronize on the same drop.

❖ Build problems force the team to confront issues they'd prefer to ignore. If team = software, then the current build is the current state of the team. Whenever I come across a project that's having trouble shipping, I always ask, "You're building this thing?" Almost invariably the response is something like, "Well, it takes so much time to build it. We build it every couple of weeks (or months or never). We're an exception to the regular, frequent builds rule because of *x*."

And yes, there are many difficulties in achieving regular builds, but they're difficulties that if solved yield a much healthier team and a smoother process. The discipline imposed on the developer, who must check for functionality and lack of regression before he or she can integrate a component into the master code, for instance, greatly reduces the costliness of coding flaws.

It's easy to be delusional when you're creating software, but in the face of the daily build, much potential for fantasy is harmlessly discharged.

#33:   *Get to a known state and stay there.*

This is a conceptually simple yet extremely powerful idea. The corollary is, "Have a shippable product every day."

Get to a known state and stay there. You pretty much know what your product is when you ship it. By the time you ship it, you know what kind of shape it's in, as much as you're ever going to know that—architecture, features, performance characteristics, and so on. At the time you ship the product, you have the fewest unknowns.

If you ask a developer the status of something he's working on, his answer might be correct, but if it is, that's just a coincidence.

Now, suppose someone asked you to add one little feature to the product you've just shipped. That request would be something that you could grasp, that you'd feel confident you could do. You'd understand the implications, and you could visualize the process you'd use. You definitely know how to add a single feature to a shipped product. You'd call together a program manager, a QA person, a developer, and a documenter. You'd all develop an understanding of the new feature. All would have clear visions of their roles and contributions in the creation of this feature, and you'd say, "Now go play."

In short order, in a few days probably, or at most a week or two, the feature team would return, diskette in hand, with the new version of the software containing its single new feature. The process isn't at all difficult.

That's the idea of getting to a known state and staying there. Think of developing a new release as just a continuous process of adding many single features to a known product and shipping it out the door as it was. That's the most helpful way to understand and organize software development activities. Organize multidisciplinary feature teams and have them add features one at a time to an understood product. The key is to always keep the product in a known, shippable state. Never let the product become a bunch of bits piling up on the floor. Never let it unravel completely. Keep it tight. Keep it happening. Once you get it to a known state, keep it there.

Don't try to do this without a QA group. It won't work without a QA group. You've got to have someone whose job it is to articulate status. If you ask a developer the status of something he's working on, his answer might be correct, but if it is, that's just a coincidence. The developers are in the middle of it. They don't know what the real status of the product is. Someone else has to assess and articulate status, someone with a different mind-set, someone whose job in life is to articulate the state of things.

And have some little tests that you run every day—say, a little automated test and some hand tests. Then conduct full product sweeps weekly or biweekly. And see that every day your product is in a shippable state.

What is a known state? A known state is a state in which you have accurate status information about all components at a given point in time. You know that your information about the product is accurate because the product's status has been tested by QA. The status consists of a comprehensive list of tested and missing functionality, bug count sorted by severity, bug arrival rate, bug fix rate, projected total bug count, and the other vital metrics.

The moment of ship-worthiness in a product development cycle is evident to everyone involved.

We look for numbers. Churn is a great number, too. We measure the amount of change in the code day to day, how much we are churning. There are various numbers you can use, but the point is, whatever numbers you use, you use them every day.

No, it isn't QA's job to determine when a product is ready to ship. The moment of ship-worthiness in a product development cycle is evident to everyone involved, and it's non-controversial. Shipping has been the goal of the entire effort. Crossing the finish line, while it has intangible emotional and definite financial rewards, is no surprise when you've observed every single painful step toward it.

But the only reason you've been able to make these micro-observations is that you got to a known state and you stayed there. And your QA group is how you did it.

Achieving a relatively accurate view into product status is a challenging feat, requiring a highly motivated and competent QA team. Many software development organizations have rudimentary or no real QA, and they can't do much in the way of assessment until they make the appropriate investments in creating a modern development organization.

You Gotta Be Able to Mark Your Progress

The following section, more than any other in this book, describes the nitty-gritty details of the development process I have variously followed, created, stolen, adopted, or begged for. Many brilliant minds and numerous huge mistakes have been invested in getting it this far. The core is Rule #33, above, "Get to a known state and stay there." The consistent application of frequent milestones and all of the attendant learning and progress stem from that basic idea.

You want to get somewhere with your software, you want to make progress, so you need to set markers up along the chronological way and try to reach them. We call these markers "milestones."

A milestone without a mechanism to track progress is a milestone unlikely to be met. Don't have any goal you haven't precisely defined. Make very specific contracts for each and every little goal. Invest in clarity.

#34: *Use ZD milestones.*

A software product under construction is inherently invisible: partially, it hangs out in the minds of its creators; partially, it gets congealed in impenetrable bits and words and plans scattered about in machinery and on paper; and partially it is wholly unknown, withheld from human ken until all the software specters have manifested themselves and been dealt with, each in its turn. Software is at least partially a product of the collective unconscious of the team, and at any given time various unconscious group drives—both creative and pathological—are expressing themselves in the group's daily activity and in the individual and communal choices they make. As we've noted, the software product is in effect a projection of the team, so software will inevitably express the true state of the team that created it. All you need to know about the state of any software development team is revealed to you by the state of their product.

> **"Zero defects" doesn't mean that there are no bugs in the software, or that it has no missing functionality.**

If software development activity is to be managed, the product must be periodically forced to the surface, where all of the team's efforts to date can be scrutinized and the effects of their creative or pathological drives analyzed. And the information that becomes available when the entire product under construction is forced to the surface as a united whole, or artifact, provides the basis for the team's further efforts. But while the benefits of causing a product to surface are many, achieving insight into the product, the process, and the underlying drives of the team is a complex undertaking.

Regardless of that complexity, in order to function properly, the team need to get their bearings, consolidate their gains, and muster the courage to face their troubled areas. They need to heighten their awareness of their state,

> **Shipping the product is just the last milestone in the project.**

increase their confidence in their ability to predict effort and results, and renew their confidence that their vision—worked out so painstakingly in earlier team efforts (see Rule #3, "Create a multi-release technology plan")—is slowly but surely materializing.

Many of the groups at Microsoft get their bearings via a mechanism called *ZD milestones.* "ZD" stands for "zero defects," although that doesn't mean that there are no bugs in the software, or that it has no missing functionality. At a ZD milestone, the team achieve the quality level set for the milestone in the time allotted to meet it, and the product is tested to that effect. In our Visual C++

group, we typically have three or four ZD milestones per product, where a normal product cycle might run a year.

Shipping the product is just the last milestone in the project. Shipping is of course the coolest milestone, but it's really no more important than the three or four milestones that preceded it.

Rule #33, "Get to a known state and stay there," advocates bringing your product to a shippable condition, and keeping it in a shippable condition, each and every day, forevermore. That, at least, is the ideal; but it's important to recognize that you're going to miss achieving that ideal much of the time. This is because you have to do regressive things—say, removing major sections of working code for alteration—or artificial things, like temporarily stubbing in new functionality. By putting the ZD milestone concept to work, though, you catch up on the principle of constantly maintaining a shipping product.

The team might work for six weeks or two months on a milestone, and then, when they reach the predetermined milestone date, not proceed with any further development activity of any type until the original goals of the milestone have been achieved. Generally, the goals of the milestone are expressed (among other ways) in terms of deliverables, things to be handed from one person to another. When all the deliverables have been certifiably delivered, the current milestone is achieved and work on the next milestone begins.

This principle is much more simply stated than realized. If you have an "empowered development team," deliverables are negotiated among developers, writers, program managers, and testers. "Management" has virtually nothing to say about deliverables. Each deliverable has associated with it a quality criterion that can be objectively verified by QA. The acceptance criteria are expressed in specific detail and agreed to in advance. All the planned deliverables that can be targeted to a particular moment of time are aggregated, primarily by program managers, into the milestone.

A key benefit of using ZD milestones is that you can monitor slips close to when they happen. If you must hit a milestone every few months, the most slippage you can incur is the slippage at the current milestone. You know how much you're slipping at intervals much shorter than the whole project's duration. When you get to a milestone date and the product is nowhere in sight, you have some good information. And when the product finally achieves the milestone goals, n weeks late, you are in a position to say, "Well, I can't tell you how much we've slipped the rest of the schedule, but we're off by n weeks at this point."

#35: *Nobody reaches the ZD milestone until everybody does.*

If one group is having more difficulty than another, instead of letting the slower group struggle unaided while the faster group proceeds with development, the program manager asks the faster group to stop and help the slower group. The team has to do some load balancing. It does no good to have part of a product done, after all.

A truly frightening prospect (and I have seen this happen!) is that the faster group, perceiving that the slower group is critical path and thus likely to delay the product or the milestone, might proceed to add more features to their part of the product! If this kind of thing is not to go on, the entire team must be held accountable for reaching the milestone.

#36: *Every milestone deserves a no-blame postmortem.* _____

Immediately following the achievement of a milestone, conduct a postmortem on it. You can ask such timeless questions as, "How in the hell did we miss it by a hundred percent when we thought we were on top of it?" A good postmortem doesn't need to be acrimonious or particularly expensive. Program managers can conduct meetings among the feature teams, or solicit e-mail and consolidate observations into lessons learned. Especially useful is highlighting the things done well. The milestone postmortem is the mechanism by which learning is consolidated and institutionalized.

It's self-defeating to punish people in any way for being late on any milestone. The only purpose of even discussing lateness is to bring about appropriate action and instill a sense of urgency in the team about to be late, or to develop communal insight into steps that could have remediated the lateness if the slip has already happened. The only punitive consequence of lateness should stem from its actual effects on business rather than from management judgment and disapproval. Lateness often means costs of some sort for the business, and the business must ultimately compensate for these costs in some way. It would be naive of the team to expect that no costs should ever accrue to them. The team's awareness of an inevitable reckoning is sufficient negative motivation.

Blame in these circumstances is silly. You might as well blame the leaves for falling.

This is not to say that delivering something later than expected is not something that is ever brought up to an individual as possible fodder for a career development discussion. But generally speaking, in the healthy team at any rate, people are on top of lateness, behave more or less optimally in correcting for it, are constantly tweaking expectations, and are themselves expected to reach in their efforts to begin with, whence risk and complexity arise in the first place. Blame in these circumstances is silly. You might as well blame the leaves for falling.

If you cause enough introspection in your team over a number of milestones, and if they learn and incorporate the lessons from their own mistakes, the team will eventually reach the point of maturity at which they will start to hit milestones, one right after the other.

#37: *Stick to both the letter and the spirit of the milestone.*

Milestones are expensive, and they can be painful, but they are the only way to ensure success. The expense comes from the difficult and sometimes agonizing negotiations over what will be delivered to whom and in what shape at the milestone. The pain comes from the self-imposed discipline, trimming features to achieve the milestone. And the pain comes from the difficulty of getting everybody to focus on the milestone, to cooperate on creating its values, and to put in the extra effort to achieve it, even though shipping might be months or more than a year away.

The insurance that ZD milestones provide more than compensates for the expense and pain of their construction and for the meticulous postmortem you must subject each one to. By using ZD milestones, you bring integrity into your evaluation of process early, and you sustain the integrity of your evaluations throughout the project. Comprehending reality becomes the highest team value because so many interpersonal and group commitments are being made and either kept or broken. When the content of a milestone is defined at the milestone's onset, expectations are set. The credibility of the milestone derives from the buy-in, the large number of individual promises.

As an early milestone's feature content evolves and time passes, the team's awareness of the extent of their commitments and the shortage of time forces them to examine the integrity of the milestone, the sense in which they'll be able to meet it, whether they'll really meet it. I've been involved in several milestone experiences in which the team concluded that they would meet the "letter" but not the "spirit" of an early milestone. This scrupulousness is noteworthy. In my experience, a healthy team is always sensitive to the integrity issue. A good team are wary of deceiving themselves. This truthtelling implies that people must be able to speak their minds and that no rigid conventional wisdom can rule the team. Free speech is "openers" for successful software development practice. I've heard team members challenge each other not to chisel on the feature list for an early milestone. They can smell each other (and themselves) weaseling out of commitments.

> **I've heard team members challenge each other not to chisel on the feature list for an early milestone.**

It's perfectly acceptable to remove features from an early milestone, or to reduce quality expectations, or to change dates or add resources. It's a fatal mistake, however, not to confront the issues that give rise to the need for such compensation, for therein lies the growth of the team. Only by doing this self-examination early in the product development cycle will the team grow enough to succeed in the later, arguably more critical, milestones.

#38: *Get a handle on "normal."*

What are the fundamental characteristics of an M1 milestone, an M2 milestone, and so on? Without a firm sense (or definition) of normative behavior for each kind of milestone, you'll find it impossible to identify pathological behavior during a milestone. The leadership and the team are then left without the tools they need to affirm the team's well-being or diagnose its symptoms. Prognosis, intervention, and remediation are impossible without a good sense of what is normal.

Diagnostics

One of the most difficult (and rewarding) activities in any software development project is to correctly evaluate the behavior of the team and the state of the product at various points in time. Because the experience of creating software is so dynamic, so filled with fits of angst and bursts of joy, so downright unpredictable, it is often extremely difficult to tell whether some behavior, or team mood, or schedule slippage, or other apparently negative event is normal or pathological. This lack of certainty makes it difficult to prescribe remedial or alternative behaviors with any confidence.

Once upon a time, for example, a team I was a part of was about to miss the first milestone (M1) in a very aggressive schedule on an extremely full-featured product. The stakes for us were enormously high, and while our team was generally confident, we were also aware that our past performance was no guarantee of future success, that the great god of software can humble any group of humans at whim.

The Featuritis Diagnosis

During this M1 period, the team had been dogged by one particularly pernicious symptom of software development ill-health: featuritis. It had become apparent to us early in the milestone period that a few key components, particularly those in support of our paradigm shifts (see Rule #3, "Create a multi-release technology plan," and the box "Refining the Technology Plan"), didn't have enough reach to support the messages we wanted to send about our product when it was released. The inadequacy of these components had led to some intense introspection, debate, management screw-ups, and team dislocations. These in turn had ultimately led to a vibrant new design that added significantly to the work of virtually all teams—and about which virtually everybody was enthused.

This process of change for the better was not without its difficult ripple effects: for three weeks during the milestone period, the team didn't know whether the new proposed central features would be in the product; whether

(continued)

Featuritis

painful feature trade-offs were imminent, and if so, who would be working on what; how those decisions were going to be made and who would make them when; whether we would be able to reclaim our fragile and expensively won consensus and clarity of purpose; whether management would adhere to its oft-expressed promise of team empowerment (especially since some of the leaders and managers were advocating the new features). The list of questions and uncertainties went on and on. It shouldn't be difficult to see how these concerns might have distracted us from our focus on achieving the goals of the M1 we'd first defined.

Featuritis—the nonconsensual addition or elaboration of features—is very debilitating, even without reference to the ultimately greater workload it creates. In our discussions, though, it became clear to us that we weren't even sure we were suffering from featuritis—even though we had added features during a milestone period, which broke one of our own cardinal rules. Yes, the data strongly suggested that we were being undisciplined, but we had thoroughly investigated each proposed new feature, analyzed its impact on everyone and everything, and achieved a new consensus that it was an essential feature and that not having it in the original plan was a serious design flaw to begin with. We had concluded that by trading around other features and reallocating staff we could in fact do each of the new features without significant schedule impact or risk.

Now, however, we were faced with the consequences of this defocusing decision process: after turning away from the great feature debate and getting back to developing the software and meeting our milestone, we saw that M1 was unmistakably and significantly in danger. In an assembly of all the program managers and some of the other leads throughout the business unit, including the head of QA, we assessed our status. The discussion that ensued fully expressed both the fundamental unknowability of software development and its absolute manageability. I love it.

The Arguments

Several people argued that we could readily make M1 by trimming our expectations of precisely what the planned M1 features were; it was not that we wouldn't deliver particular features, but that they would perhaps not be as comprehensive as we had idealistically first envisioned them—although precisely what was envisioned was debatable to begin with, this being the first milestone. These people felt we could still meet the letter of the milestone if not the spirit.

(continued)

A second group argued that this was not a fair characterization, that in fact the spirit of the milestone had not been thoroughly defined in the first place, and that even the letter was subject to various interpretations. While they were basically in support of the proposition that M1 could be met, these people objected to the "sullying" of the achievement, to saying that we were somehow violating the milestone even as we met it.

A third camp was aghast at our behavior to date. They felt that we had improperly allowed significant features to be added during the milestone itself and that now we were trying to weasel out of the costs thus incurred by chiseling on the deliverables. Their basic argument was that in claiming to "meet" the M1 milestone on any terms at this point, we were deluding ourselves, pretending that we were disciplined, fully cognizant, and full of integrity, when in fact we were software wussies, lacking the backbone to either control our featuritis or admit (and confront) our deficiencies with respect to M1.

In the course of the discussion, someone pointed out that we were not suffering from featuritis at all, that featuritis is a different sort of beast altogether from the one that tormented us. Featuritis is the unconscious, nonconsensual addition of features, primarily small ones, that are never brought to the surface for genuine consensus building. The scope of such features is less than or equal to some perceived "standard" size, so they are winked at and acknowledged as inevitable. As features of this type mount up, their cumulative effect is to inhibit the timely meeting of milestones. Escaping detection, these little features ultimately delay deployment of the product.

Often, as disease will strike any debilitated organism, featuritis attacks the team who are behind in the market or who otherwise have a losing image—and self-image. In the healthy team, the idea of slipping a ship date for a feature provokes a natural abhorrence that only a zealous and legitimate belief in the importance of the new feature can overcome. The team's immune system functions less well in times of great uncertainty or defeatism, rendering it more susceptible not only to featuritis but to a host of other software plagues. With every wind in the market or ripple among the customers, such a team frantically add to and redefine the product, unconsciously certain of their ultimate failure.

The features we were adding to M1, however, had been exhaustively analyzed, and consensus on the need for change had been painstakingly built from the ground up. All key members of the team had agreed that if we had to we would slip the product schedule for these features. The features we were adding were integral to our paradigm-shifting effort, and without them it was certain we would fail to change the way people work. The impact on the schedule and the team had been anticipated. All cross-functional teams were in essential agreement that the wisest course was to pursue developing the features.

Just M1-ness

The conclusion of the great M1 argument is noteworthy. The team decided that what we were experiencing was inherent "M1-ness," as opposed to some software development pathology. We declared that we were free from featuritis because we had so thoroughly done our due diligence—an activity that precluded the featuritis diagnosis. Further, the team unanimously decided that the vagaries of the M1 deliverables, especially their malleability, stemmed more from the "M1-ness" of our situation than from any lack of discipline or intellectual rigor.

Basically, we realized that M1 was the time in any project during which this sort of thing gets worked out, that the purpose of having an M1 is to resolve design ambiguities, discover scheduling weaknesses, and fully commit the team to a particular refined product vision. The conclusion—surprising in its unanimity and in the vehemence with which it was expressed—was that we were on track for M1, that all the goals we could possibly hope to achieve were being achieved, that there was no particular behavior that we wanted from the team that was different from the behavior we were experiencing.

#39: *A handful of milestones is a handful.*

All that said, it's generally best to schedule a milestone somewhere between every six weeks and every three months. With smaller, feature, teams (say, 10 to 20 people total), you can have more frequent milestones because smaller teams reduce the overhead of a milestone. Small teams and frequent milestones can yield more rapid growth and enculturation, too. (See Rule #7: "Use feature teams.")

But any project that has more than seven milestones (or so) is suspect, in my view, or at least extraordinary. People can't project reality that many milestones into the future. My experience suggests that three or four milestones plus the ship milestone are an optimal number. (Also see Rule #18: "Cycle rapidly.")

A Handful of Milestones

#40: *Every little milestone has a meaning (story) all its own.* ⎯⎯⎯⎯⎯⎯

Each milestone needs a story. Recall that in my team's discussion of whether we were meeting M1, there was considerable debate over whether we were meeting the spirit of the milestone as well as the letter of the milestone. The spirit of a milestone can be expressed in the story of the milestone. The story is a one- or two-sentence description of what is meant to be achieved in the milestone. All arguments can be resolved (theoretically) by reference to the milestone story. The story also articulates the goal. The reason I don't call it the milestone goal is that it must have the dynamics and the moral, the message, of a story. It must ultimately encapsulate the meaning of the milestone. Most humans don't find it motivating or rewarding to achieve a goal as purely abstract as something called M1, an immaterial list of deliverables we have convinced ourselves represents progress (something we could be totally wrong about—remember, this is software). A list just won't engage the emotions, the focus, and the intensity required to deliver great software. People will make sacrifices to achieve something meaningful. They will invest their souls and their energies in visible, concrete results.

I have found several milestone stories useful in the context of Visual C++. In a typical M1 milestone, we usually aim to achieve a capability we call "dogfooding." Dogfooding is using the product under development to further your development effort. The idea stems from the old marketing saw, popularized at Microsoft by Steve Ballmer, that dogfood manufacturers should "eat their own dogfood." For a development tool like Visual C++, this concept is particularly important since Visual C++ is created with Visual C++. For our team to achieve 100 percent dogfooding means that our new version must be more productive than the old version, even given the new version's incompleteness and bugginess. We will not generally enforce dogfooding: managers will not run around coercing people to use the current product version. However, the entire team is aware that dogfooding is an important sign of progress, that if we can get to a dogfood status for all components, everything will go better. By constantly using the product, we'll find more bugs and deficiencies, gain more productivities, and realize more design efficiencies.

Giving out our new versions is something we do selectively.

Another theme (and a most telling element) in our milestone story–making is when we are willing to give what to whom. We are protective of our reputation, and giving out our new versions is something we do selectively. And giving things out at the wrong times can substantially increase the workload of the team. A milestone might thus be defined by when you give your product to "early customers."

So the story for our M1 milestone might be something like, "All components will be dogfooded by the majority of the team, and we will release the build tools to friendly internal Microsoft sites." This would naturally be shortened to "dogfooding and internal customers." A story for a later milestone—say, the third—might be "all features complete, visual freeze [no changes to the user interface], deliveries to a handful of friendly external sites."

The key points about milestone stories are

❖   The story encodes the spirit of the milestone.

❖   Success is judged by whether the milestone story has been fulfilled.

❖   The team understand and consent to the milestone story before they launch the milestone effort.

#41:   *Look for the natural milestones.*

While it's difficult to delineate precisely when—that is, in which milestone—certain normal things must happen, it is clear that there are certain organic, or natural, milestones that take place during any normal software development effort that's headed toward the achievement of great software. No, "normal" doesn't mean "common." By "normal," I mean the things that will naturally happen in a team free of notable software development neurosis or psychosis. Certain events must happen before great software can be delivered:

1. The design stabilizes.

2. The deliverables become crisp.

3. The team realizes the "true" extent of the effort required to finish. (This ordinarily happens many times, usually as the result of slippages.)

4. The design is shrunk, or resources are added, or the schedule slips—usually all three.

5. Development activity ceases.

6. The product enters and exits a debug/stabilization phase.

These six "natural" milestones occur not only in the large—across the whole of the product development cycle—but also in the small—within each milestone. I discuss these natural milestones at some length below, but note here that each milestone behaves the same way as all the milestones together behave, which in turn (in the best of all possible worlds) behave the same way as the entire technology plan behaves.

Healthy team behavior during each natural milestone period has a predictable pattern. It is this pattern of behavior, which I call the metamilestone pattern, that managers should watch for and constantly nurture. If the metamilestone pattern is not emerging, the manager should presume unhealthy behavior and take remedial action. The pattern as far as I have analyzed it consists of the six events. How long each event lasts is not precisely predictable. The surest sign that one event is over is the emergence of the next, but note that some events can happen with near simultaneity. Whether the events occur more serially or more in parallel is largely determined by the bandwidth of team communications because these events travel through the team like a virus.

1. The design stabilizes. Initially most feature designs (and product designs) are abstractions about which everybody is simultaneously enthused and confused. Team members are enthusiastic because each person is projecting his or her vision of the particular feature into the design. They are confused for the same reason. All are agreed (given the technology planning and consensus building that has gone on before the milestone work is launched) that the feature is exactly what ought to be done; yet, when challenged, no one knows precisely what activities ought to be done by whom, and when. What I call "the software dream syndrome" (more on that later) is usually at work here. And awakening to an absence of detail will be progressive and repetitious.

"Oh, yeah," says the developer, "we're definitely adding foobars in the first milestone. I'm working out how they'll look and behave right now."

Or, says the QA lead, "Widgets are kicking in during M2. Definitely. But how exactly they're supposed to work I don't know."

Traditionally, at least in more disciplined organizations, software development activity has proceeded from some combination of requirements documents, written specifications, or graphical depictions of program logic and design composed before the actual commencement of the project. While these lists, specs, and charts can remedy to a large extent the early absence of detail, I'm opposed to spending time on them for several reasons:

❖ Rapid change inevitably overtakes the original specification. Keeping the spec up-to-date becomes a moral or a bureaucratic rather than a practical necessity.

❖ Adherence to a rapidly aging design document constrains flexibility, causes opportunities to be missed, and overloads the healthy team with process.

❖ In this approach, all unknowns must be eliminated before development commences, whereas ideally the elimination of all unknowns should yield the product itself, the elimination of unknowns marking the end of development, not its beginning.

The important thing is not that you achieve what you said you were going to achieve before development got under way, but that you achieve the maximum possible given the various constraints on time and resources, and that you've selected wisely from the various design alternatives that became visible in the course of the project.

In any event, the design must stabilize and be communicated throughout the team as appropriate, through some combination of e-mail, specs, prototypes, hallway conversations, whiteboarding, and implementation. As the design clarifies, the second event should be getting under way. A manager can assess the state of things by "drilling down" into some aspect of the design and checking out whether all functional areas of the team are similarly aware of it. If they are, you can expect the second event imminently; otherwise, phase one is still immature.

2. The deliverables become crisp. "Crispness" when applied to deliverables is meant to suggest clarity, simplicity, and credibility. Expressed negatively, a crisp set of deliverables lacks ambiguity and complexity and doesn't tax credulity. At the beginning of a project and at the beginning of any milestone, deliverables are seldom crisp in these senses. Exactly what they are, when they'll be done, who will do them, and in what order are usually estimates. The estimates will be true, in the sense that an impressionist painting is true, but they will not be accurate in the sense that a photograph is accurate.

As the design stabilizes and the QA, program management, development, and documentation specialists on the feature team begin to comprehend it more concretely, they are progressively in a position to more specifically describe their needs and objectives. Communication among the team members soars as a common vocabulary about the design emerges, its scope is commonly understood, and its sequence of development becomes clear to everyone. At this point, negotiations re-open and detail is sketched into the schedule.

3. The team realizes the "true" extent of the effort required to finish. There is of course never any genuine appreciation of the "true" amount of effort required to finish until you are finished; however, after the design has solidified and the crispness of the deliverables is emerging, a recognizable disillusionment sets in among the team members. First of all, the feature itself seems less beautiful than the team had imagined it would be. Second, it's obvious now that there's a hell of a lot more to do to achieve these crisp deliverables than the team thought. Finally, the team realizes that they need more resources, or less product, or more time—or some of all three.

At this point in all milestone work, no matter how experienced the team and their leadership, depression, a sense of impending doom, and widespread feelings of being overwhelmed surface from within the team and spread. This is a good sign, revealing advances in the team's awareness. One true manifestation of growing awareness is growing discomfort; becoming aware is basically a process of disillusionment. In the healthy team, this period of realization will climax with some sort of call to action. In our group, we usually have what we call a "war room meeting," in which the leadership of the team convenes after hours to review the situation and develop a consensual plan of action.

> **Depression, a sense of impending doom, and widespread feelings of being overwhelmed surface from within the team and spread.**

The central thing that has happened during these first three events of the metamilestone pattern is that the appropriate unknowns have been resolved. And since unknowns are seldom resolved in a way that makes things easier than expected, the increased information is frightening to the team. The healthy team will confront and overcome this fear.

4. The design is shrunk, or resources are added, or the schedule slips—or all three. The team pull out the old triangle (see Rule #28, "Remember the triangle: Features, Resources, Time") and work out the conflicts inherent in their naively constructed milestone schedule. Ideally, they are still in the first quarter (or so) of the milestone (or the project). There is good reason to believe that the healthier a team is, the more quickly the team will pass through the first three metamilestone events. The healthy team has sufficient reaction time to manipulate the triangle and rebuild consensus, this time for the revised milestone plan.

Ideally, the milestone story or the project story remains intact, although some expected aspect of the milestone might be sacrificed. Usually, numerous small aspects of the milestone are sacrificed or adjusted: a minor feature here, a bit of testing there; adding a resource here; moving the date just a smidgen there.

Until development has ceased, there is no guarantee that you are ever going to reach the milestone.

The healthy team will at this juncture demonstrate the flexibility and responsiveness that will enable them to—more or less—hit their milestone. You don't want to see milestone schedule slippage as the sole compensator. Nor do you want to see exclusively the clamor for additional resources. What you really need to see is a team earnestly working out dozens of small compromises and efficiencies in order to achieve the most effective milestone behavior possible.

5. Development activity ceases. At some point, all coding stops. The milestone is feature complete. There will necessarily be a moment when no more creation for the milestone is required or permitted and achieving stability is the only task left before achieving the milestone. This much is obvious. It's worth noting this event as a distinct metamilestone event, however, because development estimates can be infinitely wrong. Until development has ceased, there is no guarantee that you are ever going to reach the milestone.

6. The product enters and exits a debug/stabilization phase. It's fairly easy to determine approximately how late you're going to be for the milestone (or the project) if you know your net bug fix capacity (bug fix rate − bug find rate) and your net bug fix capacity is a positive number. You can also roughly predict a rate of reduction in your bug find rate on the basis of your experience with past projects of a similar nature. At this point in any milestone, reading tea leaves is *de rigueur.* How many bugs are there? How long will it take us to find and fix them? What will be our regression rate?

When these kinds of questions are under serious discussion, you are probably in the end stages of the milestone (or the project). All the integration bugs show up at this point. Bug triage (see Rule #51, "Triage ruthlessly") becomes a grim affair as the fixing of defects that would have been fixed in a more relaxed atmosphere is postponed with brutal decisiveness.

#42:   *When you slip, don't fall.* _____

Slipping is OK. Slipping is not the end of the world. Like a fever, it's uncomfortable, but it's the sign that the body is healing itself.

Here's another take on slipping. Slipping is like waking up from that software dream, getting closer to reality. "Now I see." Slipping is a part of the process of successive approximations in a bizarre, multi-level dreaming experience. You wake up from one level, and you think, "Well, *now* I'm awake. How could I have missed

So compulsive is this moralistic tendency that you'll have to resist this pressure with all your might.

the obvious fact for the last three months that there was no hope in hell of getting the *foobar* done on time? Gee, boy, now I'm awake."

Three months later, of course, or three weeks later, you realize something else that should have been totally obvious but managed utterly to escape your detection. "Wow," you say, "now I'm *really* awake. Now I see." And so on. With each "awakening," you take another step toward an absolute reality, although of course you can never be certain you won't "awaken" from the current reality. And inevitably, you do.

You can try to see this recurrent awakening as a process of growth. Certainly, each new level of awareness adds to your store of knowledge and experience, and the process tends to create a much richer environment overall. The counter to that positive view is that you always start over on each new project, at the zeroth reality level. The counter-counter-argument, of course, is that although each project starts out at the zeroth level, you, personally, are starting out at the (zero + n)th level, where n = the number of levels you've experienced (survived) to date.

In any case, navigating during these periodic awakenings, which are more often than not accompanied by slips, is hazardous but possible. These practices help during the onset of a slip:

❖ Remember that a slip has no moral dimension. It's not about failure or blame. It's the inevitable consequence of creating intellectual property. Get rid of all moral baggage associated with slipping, and insist that the rest of the team behave likewise. Because people are so frightened of being judged negatively by authority figures and crave praise, there will be substantial neurotic pressure to drag the discussion and, indeed, the entire process, of slipping, back and forth between the poles of fault and credit, blame and praise. So compulsive is this moralistic tendency that you'll have to resist this pressure with all your might.

❖ Don't hide out. Overcome the natural instinct among humans to avoid problems, conflicts, and hazards. As the team realizes it's in difficulties, they, like you, will want to avoid the repercussions. But it's during a slip that good leadership makes all the difference. Don't cower in your office, the door closed, muttering to yourself, "I'm not going out there! There's a slip going on out there!" Throw open the door and bravely proceed to the corridors and offices that are at the heart of the slip.

❖ Use a slip to provoke effective behavior. Since awareness of an impending slip is an awakening, people on the team are alive to new insights, fresh information, alternative views, and previously unimagined possibilities. Focus your own attention on the most effective response to the slip, regardless of orthodoxy or other conventional restraints. Slipping is a time of flexibility. Exploit that.

Slipping isn't the problem. Being surprised by slipping is the problem. A slip doesn't say that the product is too hard to develop. Being surprised by a slip says that the organization is broken. People aren't thinking. People aren't talking to each other. People aren't aware of the global situation.

Use your slips. You can actually gain a leadership position over the team at the moment of the slip, when they're vulnerable. That's when they're listening. That's when they want to learn. If you're yelling or crying or hiding in your office, you're missing your best opportunity to lead and to gain credibility. When you say, "OK, we've slipped. Let's have a review . . . so we'll start the review at five o'clock tonight. And we'll just go until we've reviewed every bit." They'll realize that the review is "when I get to show that I have my stuff together and that I sort of know what I'm doing." In the review, all the details of the product surface. We get it all out on the table. We look at it, fiddle with it, kick the tires. That's when slipping is a great experience for the team.

A Slip Processed

The concept of hitting a milestone is necessarily an elastic one. Milestones are never "hit" in a purely objective sense. The fluidity of feature definition, the intangibility of quality, and the tolerance for date ranges conspire to make milestone achievement a judgment call. The optimal time to declare a milestone victory is when there are diminishing returns in lingering further and the demands of the milestone story have been met. Of course, identifying that moment is difficult. The principal guidance I can offer is much like the traffic directions that go, "When you get to the Baptist church, you've gone too far." If you're near the end of the allotted milestone time and you haven't ceased all development activity, for example, you've gone too far. As a leader, you must be constantly aware of the stages the work needs to pass through and identify the minimum set of activities that will get things to the next stage.

Once upon a time (did I say "once"?), our team approached an M1 milestone and things looked pretty bleak. We were only a couple of weeks away from the date, and the case shaped up this way.

Bug counts were too high. While the number of bugs per developer was arguably reasonable, in the aggregate the number of bugs was frightening. Additionally, the number we were finding daily seemed to suggest that stabilization was far from imminent.

(continued)

Daily builds were inconsistent. (See Rule #32, "If you build it, it will ship.") While most of the product components were successfully building every day, a few components remained intransigently unbuildable. Although these components would superficially compile and link, they consistently failed the sniff tests designed to assert successful building. These failures would trigger significant delays as the sniff tests themselves and then the component source code were analyzed. When the particulars of each problem had finally been wrestled to the ground, a day or more would have been lost. (Remember, at this late stage of the milestone, a single day meant ten percent of our entire resources remaining for the milestone.)

There was no palpable sense of urgency among the team and their leadership. Usually, right before achieving a significant software goal, our team were aware of the effort they were expending. In this case, many team members were saying that things "didn't feel right." The sense seemed to be that the drive and focus characteristic of a milestone end were missing.

Communications breakdowns were common, and preventable inefficiencies seemed to be the order of the day. Glitches that were small in and of themselves were rippling through the team. One check-in would change the basis of a second check-in, causing the second to fail unexpectedly. This is a common software problem. Team A references (depends on) Team B's component. Team A's component is assembled, tested, and checked in, expecting the behavior of Team B's component to remain as it was in version N. Naturally, Team B is simultaneously checking in version N+1, which has small but crucial differences, differences Team B is sure won't bother Team A (to the extent that Team B has thought about that at all). Of course, the differences bring Team A to a standstill in the daily build because Team A had run its preliminary tests using Team B's version N.

Time for a Radical Focus on the Problem?

The first thing that will occur to the typical leader or program manager in an unpromising situation like this one is to jump into action—call out the cavalry and take the hill. And that might be an appropriate response if several factors don't mitigate against such a call to action. First of all, it costs a great deal to jump into action. While it is surely possible and often necessary to dramatically focus the team's attention on their status and risk—I call this exercise "radical focus"—you are spending a significant leadership bullet when you do. You can't clamor about the frightening state of things too often, or you'll give rise to the "cry wolf" syndrome.

Software projects are constantly slipping and in danger. This is the normal state of affairs. The only time you want to use your leadership position to explicitly instill a sense of urgency in the team is when the project is in mortal danger and needs immediate radical focus. Radical focus can be brought to bear on any given project only a few times, probably not more than twice, and even then, the two focusing moments should be far apart.

And when the team leadership calls for radical focus, the healthy team will legitimately experience a sense of disempowerment. "People in authority" have reached the conclusion that the state of things and their trend is not appropriate. The team rightly interpret this as a lack of respect for the team's decisions and priorities. Defenses rise, and then significant energy will have to be invested in disarming those defenses, or resentment will build up. Even the best leaders have a hard time penetrating defensiveness. Teaching someone against his or her will is possible, and so is swimming the English Channel.

Also, you risk triggering the anti-authority complexes of your best developers, some of whom may not be especially communicative (directly). They'll tend to respond by flipping the bozo bit on you. (See Rule #4, "Don't flip the bozo bit.") And of course there's always the distinct possibility that you've misgauged the mortality of the danger. If you have, the healthy team will push back at you, and you will either lose a significant amount of credibility when you recant, or lose credibility and loyalty when your ego drives you to push forward anyway. If the team members don't have the courage to push back, you'll identify your mistake only as your total inability to succeed becomes obvious.

You have to factor these costs and risks into a decision to call for radical focus. A call to radical focus will generally cost at least several team days, possibly a week, as you get the team's attention, maintain their interest, make them realize you really mean it, make them want to respond, and get some action initiated. The amount of time thus consumed will be a function of the size of the team, the availability of the team communication bandwidth, and the degree of latency of the team's ability to communicate.

The questions we asked ourselves as we staggered toward M1 were, What do we want the team to be aware of? How will we create that awareness? What behavior should result? (Incidentally, these are the questions you should ask yourself throughout a project.) What we really wanted our team to know in this case was that M1 was fast approaching and that unless we could build the entire product, we wouldn't make it. We also wanted the team to practice shipping. Finally, we wanted the team to experience the full effects of the immature teamwork we were experiencing and to come to the awareness that all were equally accountable for shipping the product—in this case, hitting the milestone.

(continued)

We decided that our initial impulse to call for radical focus was inappropriate: the danger wasn't mortal, and the risk that we were incorrect or that the team would resist the call to radical focus was significant. We decided to conserve our bullets for later emergencies.

What Is to Be Done?

It was clear to us, though, that our inability to build the product was holding up the entire enterprise and risking M1. We knew we couldn't allow this problem to persist. It was a bottleneck. Everything was getting out of sync as the ripple effects of broken builds spread throughout the team's activity. This bottleneck also explained our high number of bugs. Check-ins were delayed while the builds took longer than expected or failed altogether. Bug counts remained inflated because the repair check-ins weren't being made and too many new fixes were being made without validation of the previous crop. When the builds failed for too long, check-ins would eventually resume without reference to the build failures, and that added more variables to the already nearly insoluble problem of building the complete product. We did remain concerned that the appropriate degree of urgency was not materializing of its own accord.

Teamwork radiates. To establish global teamwork, you need to first establish local teamwork. If you can get three or four people behaving like a team, and that handful of people spans the entire product team, represents it completely in some way, that teamwork will radiate throughout the global team. Likewise, teamwork failures will express themselves in process and product breakdowns. When you're confronted with such a breakdown, it's more productive to identify and focus on its local source than on its manifestation.

It's worth describing the diagnostic and remediation process that led us to the decision to bring check-ins to a standstill while we fixed the daily builds. Three principal causes were at work in the builds' breaking: check-ins from various sub-teams that surprised the other teams and the build team, catching everyone unawares; inexperience on the build team, which was a relatively new department in QA, the build function having recently moved into QA from Development; and a persistent inability of one sub-team to get their component and its associated sniff tests in good enough shape to build regularly. What did these symptoms tell us about the team psyche?

A Look at the Team Psyche

The basic theory I described earlier, in "Opening Moves," is that virtually all software problems are traceable to the group psyche. When things go wrong, it's a symptom of dysfunctionality in the group. You have to ask yourself, What is the team saying about itself through its behavior?

In the first source of build breaks, the surprise check-ins, the team was expressing its lack of overall self-awareness: one part of the team wasn't talking to the others. Activities and daily goals were local in focus, uncoordinated, and sometimes even contradictory among the sub-teams. Each sub-team was more or less on track toward M1, but product integration was falling apart. Individual contributors were identifying excessively and exclusively with what they perceived to be their parts of the product.

The second source of build breaks was the relative inexperience of the build team. QA had no experience in doing builds. For previous projects, several senior developers in the group had assumed responsibility for monitoring the daily builds. These people from Development were technically capable of fixing virtually anything that stood in the way of a successful build. The overall team's expectations of the build group were thus very high. The senior developers who had watchdogged the builds had taken care of any problem through individual virtuosity and breadth of knowledge; the new build regime was having difficulty moving beyond the identification of build failures. In most failures, instant remediation was beyond their capabilities. And their enculturation within the team—where Development had been King—made them initially unable to firmly assign build breakages to the responsible developers and monitor corrections.

The rest of the team was therefore disappointed in the "performance" of the build group. Subtly, the rest of the team began flipping the bozo bit on the build group. Because senior developer types had made extraordinary efforts to ramrod the daily builds through, the broader team had gotten spoiled and had deluded themselves into thinking that our build issues were resolved. The goal now was to move accountability for daily quality to all personnel rather than have it be babysat by a senior developer. The build team's job was to build a quality product from quality sources, to maintain a predictable build sequence, and to identify bottlenecks and monitor their elimination. The team's reaction to this accountability was of course defensive: "the build team is unsuccessful in building the product today" vs. "our code wasn't buildable today."

(continued)

The third source of build breaks was the persistent failure of that one component of the product to stabilize sufficiently to build and pass all relevant sniff tests. Not surprisingly, this part of the product suffered from a history of neglect. Consistently shorthanded with respect to both Development and QA, living without a program manager, this area cried out for attention, in part by failing to build. The functionality represented by the failing piece of the product was important to our product but had been treated in many respects as a second-class citizen in our business unit. The business unit managers (including me) had created this situation by not securing sufficient high-quality resources to make work on the component go well. We would have to remedy this inequity. The team psyche and the product itself were expressing our caste view of the component's secondary importance.

In summary, the team had too little self-awareness and no sense of mutual accountability and the managers were failing to deliver the resources needed to shore things up. Once we'd diagnosed the problem to this extent, once we'd supplanted our knee-jerk, take-the-hill reactions with reasonable hypotheses about the observable team symptoms, we were in a position to take specific remedial steps.

Treating a Lack of Self-Awareness

It was clear to us that with respect to the lack of team self-awareness, subgroups neither communicating with one another nor working toward common goals, we needed to exploit the radiant properties of teamwork—that is, if you can solve it anywhere, it will be solved everywhere of its own accord. The logical place to start in this case was with program management. A program manager is after all a representative leader. The program manager's identification with the local team should be strong because it's from successfully leading the local team that the manager draws power, success, and security. But he or she is also a program manager, a member of the executive, and therefore should identify with the overall product, too. Everybody's business is a program manager's business.

A manager or a bureaucrat could mandate that communications should henceforward improve (!) or put a procedure in place to "encourage" more effective communications. However, trying to create (or worse, to mandate or otherwise bureaucratize) genuine and effective team communications globally is a preposterously ambitious and vain enterprise. The issues are too numerous, the number of relationships among the communicators grows exponentially, and the probability of the immediate failure of any sort of management initiative is extremely high. On the other hand, to teach or encourage two or three program managers to communicate with each other about status, goals, hopes, and both short- and long-term technology agendas, while difficult, is not impossible. If communication in such a microcosm is high-bandwidth and low-latency and transcends individual sub-team boundaries among program managers, the global teamwork will come about naturally, even rapidly, from there. What you can't create, you can foster.

While there were many program managers working on various aspects of the product, there were three who could represent the entire team by virtue of both their charters and their talents. Two were "component owners," and the third was the lead "box" guy. The box guy was the senior program manager, although he was the youngest of the three, and had shipped several products in our business unit before, while the two component owners had not been in significant leadership roles before, although they were rising stars. Communication among these three was poor. One problem was that the senior box program manager wasn't providing sufficient leadership to the two component owners, wasn't "showing them the way."

Partially, this leadership vacuum came from the fact that the three reported to three different managers. It also came from the fact that this was an M1 milestone. This early in the development project, the three program managers had an immature awareness of their individual roles and the potential of their roles. They tended to do what they thought the last people in their roles had done, or what they thought the last people should have done. And they had only narrow communications among themselves. This problem showed up as a symptom in the daily build. To unravel its pathogenesis, we had to determine how the three program managers' lack of teamwork was related to broken builds. It wasn't hard.

Scapegoating

The builds sometimes broke because the unexpected check-ins described earlier caused dependency-based cascade failures. Yet the individual program managers were of course aware of their local teams' pending check-ins. The builds also broke because the quality of the incoming code was erratic. The individual program managers should have pushed back on Development (or at least monitored QA's push-back) when sloppy code came in or good development procedures weren't followed. Instead, they themselves had begun to slip into the mentality that "the build team isn't doing their job"—localizing the phenomena and finding an appropriate scapegoat.

Scapegoating is invariably a sign of failed teamwork. It prospers in an environment with a narrow, misunderstood, or distorted sense of accountability. Individuals and groups with a strong moral ideation are especially vulnerable to scapegoatism. Typically, the person or group who is scapegoated

(continued)

A Slip Processed *continued*

symbolizes or otherwise externalizes some pathology in the team psyche. Scapegoatism is a maladaptive, defensive reaction in which failure and other evils are magically warded off by finding someone to blame. The team will find a scapegoat instinctively as a way of preserving local functionality in spite of a deteriorating general situation. Scapegoating is an attempt to simplify, localize, and, in effect, amputate an unhealthiness that is endangering the team.

Although scapegoating is a primitive, naive, and brute-force attempt at remediation, it can actually lead to small, short-term improvements in the group psyche. That's why it's so common and why it tends to survive as a practice, particularly where teams are of short-lived duration. After all, if the team is going to die anyway, short-term gains are the only kind of gains there are. Smarter, stronger people tend not to be scapegoated; weaker, younger, more vulnerable people do. Scapegoating is thus one somewhat grotesque way for the underled team to "cull the herd," although much potential is wasted in the process.

Unfortunately, scapegoating is not self-limiting. It will grow until massive inefficiencies abound and the ability to create great software and ship it on time is profoundly compromised. A sure sign of scapegoating vs. teamwork is the obliviousness of the victims to their scapegoat status. At most, they will perceive themselves as at fault for some perceived ill; but generally they'll balance this perception or repress it altogether by means of their own defenses and their own reverse scapegoatism. The purpose of scapegoating is not to identify and remediate inefficiencies but to tolerate them, even to build them in, by blaming someone else for their continuation, generally, preferably, someone beyond the scapegoater's sphere of influence. Ultimately, untreated scapegoating is fatal: it will rage through the team, their management, and their management.

The destructiveness of scapegoating goes on in two dimensions. The direct victims (the people blamed) are assigned guilt, primarily by their peers. Ostracism and disrespect toward them grows, and they respond with impenetrable defensiveness and reverse scapegoatism. Whatever their original levels of effectiveness, their effectiveness is greatly reduced by the effects of scapegoatism. The secondary victims are the balance of the team, and they are victimized in at least two ways and with more profound and dangerous consequences: since blame has been improperly though conveniently assigned, true cause and effect are never analyzed, genuine inefficiencies are never exposed, and the problems are left to express themselves in new ways that in turn trigger more scapegoating. The newly validated scapegoating impulse becomes stronger than ever, having just fed itself by taking huge bites out of the efficiency of the team. A single successful scapegoating episode will always compound the virulence of the scapegoating impulse in the rest of the team.

The second destructive dimension of scapegoating, and the more profound and dangerous one, is that the balance of the team usually suffers from the reverse scapegoating originating from the first-designated scapegoats. Then the hierarchy becomes involved (even if one must be created just to validate the scapegoating phenomenon!). There are "two sides," and "someone in authority" must adjudicate. This of course leads to diminished credibility, broken loyalties, and lack of respect for those "in authority" because there is no way to adjudicate folly or to select a correct path from among incorrect paths.

The leaders and program managers must always be aware that any scapegoating situation, especially one that's growing (and all cases of scapegoating will grow if no intervention takes place), is a serious symptom of team pathology. The long-term impact will be devastating.

In our case, the program managers had the responsibility, along with the build group, for setting the expectations of the global team: now that senior development resources would no longer support the build process, increased global accountability for the quality of the build sources should follow. For their part, the build group's principal problem had been accepting uncritically an assignment that wasn't structured for success.

In the end we decided that, given the extent of our problems, it would be optimal for the team if we missed the precise M1 date by a few days or even a week. Missing our date would allow the team to see our vulnerability expressed in concrete, unmistakable terms early in the project without our having to spend the radical focus bullet. It was clear to us that this minor slippage was unavoidable at this stage anyway and that it would serve a useful purpose as a memorable wound for the team. Inducing radical focus would have been less useful than inducing a simple focus on the problems that were blocking the daily build. Since the entire team was blocked until the build was unblocked, we decided that we had to stop flooding the build until the build team was capable of operating at the optimal rate of speed. We allowed no check-ins until the build had passed all the sniffs.

Then we ensured that the build team realized both how important their contribution was and that they had the responsibility to go back to the developers and insist that the developers fix their bugs. Finally, we put enough people on the nettlesome subcomponent that had been giving us so much trouble that it passed all its sniff tests and was successfully integrated into the build.

(continued)

Theater

How things are communicated says what they mean. A piece of e-mail with nothing special about it says that there's nothing special about the message. A team meeting is, or should be, one of the most extreme forms of communication: the subtext of a team meeting is either "this is important" or "this summons was mandated by someone other than our immediate leaders."

The decision to stop the flow of check-ins was processed by the leadership of the team in a "special war room meeting." In our particular culture, a special war room meeting—as opposed to a routine, endgame war room meeting—and one called with little notice, usually the same day, carries the subtexts that (1) the meeting concerns shipping a product, (2) one or more senior managers will probably be present, (3) the topics to be discussed are important and require consensus, and (4) all the leaders of the team had better be there. There is no mandate that anybody come, but decisions will be made with or without you. By default, the lead program manager facilitates the meeting. Generally that's the person who calls the meeting as well, but any of the leads could.

Note here the distinction between announcing a decision and processing one. If a senior manager says, "Here's what we're going to do," the rest of the team will follow (after appropriate discussion, where "appropriate" means whatever the senior manager will allow). Announcing a decision marks the closure of discussion, the end of the team's opportunity to add value to the thinking that goes into the decision. It also underlines the point that someone else is making decisions. If a team member is smarter or more creative or more informed than the person making the decisions, he or she will be frustrated and angry, and the rest of the team (and ultimately the customers) will suffer because that person wasn't able to add value.

Processing a decision in a meeting is much more effective. Usually someone (or some smaller group) has identified a significant problem, has thought it through, has consulted with several local experts about it, and has arrived at a tentative plan of action. The problem and its implications are presented and discussed informally. People in the meeting usually know that the topic is coming up, and they themselves would probably bring it up if it weren't already on the (official or unofficial) agenda. They're generally aware of the problem as central somehow, even if they haven't thought it through and have no immediate plan of action in mind. Usually in these meetings, additional ideas and useful cautionary advice get expressed, too. The tentative plan evolves, someone states the new, revised plan succinctly, and consensus is sought in a kind of vote. Participants are accountable for making themselves heard and understood and then for supporting the plan that has been processed in this fashion.

#43: *Don't trade a bad date for an equally bad date.*

Someday I'm going to retire and go off to Academia to work out the precise mathematics of slipping. I do know, though, that your biggest slip should be your first slip, and that they should get smaller and smaller until they converge on the ship date. Take your biggest lumps at the first slip.

The magnitude of a slip is directly proportional to the degree of uncertainty in the project. Since the degree of uncertainty should be getting smaller with each passing day, over time slips should get smaller. Ideally, the mathematical relationship of your slippage magnitude to your degree of uncertainty won't be some asymptotically-approaching-zero-but-never-quite-getting-there kind of thing.

I am convinced that there is an algorithm (at least in theory) that, given a couple of slips, the time frames, and the uncertainty factors, would yield a projected end date. The reason I'm convinced of this, I'm sure, has something to do with the fact that I've never tried to work it out. But you see the point: keep your eye on the size of the slips you're experiencing. The sequence of slip sizes can tell you whether the project is moving toward or away from completion.

And never trade a bad date for an equally bad date. That's a bad deal. You're just hemorrhaging credibility if you do that. Generally, you know you're going to be late before you know when you're going to be done. There comes a moment when everybody on God's green earth—everybody on the team and everybody they come in contact with—knows that you're going to be late. But the official date is still the official date. People on the team are coming up to you, saying, "Everybody knows we're late. Why don't we change the date?" The pressure to reset the end date or the milestone date is enormous. People are uncomfortable with the idea that they have a bad date. But the moment to change the date is not the moment you discover you're going to be late.

The absolute worst thing you can do is take the estimated amount of the current slip and add it to the end of your schedule. This amounts to taking the one thing you're certain is wrong (your current schedule) and putting it back in your path. This tack might seem expedient ("We won't have to think it all through

Generally, you know you're going to be late before you know when you're going to be done.

again"), but it is the apex of foolishness. The one thing you should know for sure is that you'll have to think it all through again.

Even though your information is obviously better now than when you originally set your goal, it's probably not sufficient for you to make a new schedule. It's difficult to say precisely and for all cases when you should "officially" slip your date to a new one. A good general rule is that you don't reset the schedule until the total extent of the slip is known for each component, the causes of the slip are understood, and remedies are in place. This usually takes the effort of the entire team and its leadership, and it must be an explicit, focused activity. Until you have that mathematics for slips I'm going to analyze and present to the industry in a future life, you don't know how to predict your end date. You should calibrate your closest next, near-in, milestone precisely and realistically, and you should content yourself for the moment with highlighting the continuing uncertainties about later milestones.

Take the time to stop everything and reschedule as an explicit, focused activity. Take your time. You're not going to get later by knowing where you're at. You're going to get earlier.

#44: *After a slip, hit the next milestone, no matter what.* _____

Realize that with each slip you and your team are spending credibility. It's essential that after a slip, you hit the next milestone. The team need to restore their faith in themselves, and your group need to restore their credibility in the larger context, to rebuild their stores of credibility.

After you know how bad the slip is for each component, you know what caused the slips, and you know what you need to do to fix them, create a new, closer, and more conservative milestone, one the team can't miss, and promulgate that. If you have to define the milestone as *do nothing for three weeks*, that's fine. All right, that would be a little extreme. But hit that next milestone. Redefine it, and hit it. Make it a slam-dunk affair. You can't miss that next milestone because you and the team must regain your credibility. The team need that feeling of confidence that comes with a success, that feeling of vigor, that feeling that they know what they're doing and that they can hit a milestone. That emotional dimension is important. If the team believe they can hit milestones, they start to. That just seems to be the way the human animal works.

#45: *A good slip is a net positive.* _____

Make that slip a positive experience—learn from it. Now your unknowns are becoming known. They're making themselves felt. It's time to analyze them, to wrestle them to the ground and turn them all the way into knowns. If you make a moral judgment that slipping is bad, it will get in the way of your making progress. Slipping is expected.

Although it's undesirable to have so many unknowns that slippage occurs, it's not an unusual situation—and may even be the norm. Much of contemporary software development is essentially experimental. New platforms, new operating systems, new programming technologies converge on new programming projects to create a high degree of uncertainty.

Slips are inevitable. To avoid calamity, you need to take certain measures in connection with a slip. Ideally, one or more of the pre-identified unknowns caused the slip and everybody involved understands that the risk to the schedule had been anticipated. Alternatively, everyone needs to understand how the unknowns were overlooked, and this knowledge should become part of the group knowledge for the future. You also need to determine whether people have been working on the right things. Often slips occur because members of the team have gotten preoccupied with features of marginal consequence or features that don't belong to the core product message.

If the slip was a surprise, you know that your communications system is broken and that dramatic communications efforts are required. You'll bring large amounts of detail to the surface for everybody on the team to see. You'll all assess the reality of all current near-term estimates. You'll expose denial. Slips reveal your team's weaknesses and present a good opportunity for insightful management and mentoring. Make sure that each individual who has a role in the slip receives the guidance and support he or she needs.

A slip is also an opportunity to re-evaluate feature content and resource loads, generally with an eye toward decreasing the features and shoring up deficient areas on the team.

A good slip should be a net positive.

#46: *See the forest.*

If six components are each 90 percent certain to hit a milestone, you have a total of only 53 percent certainty of hitting the milestone ($.9^6$). Everyone's being 90 percent certain is thus a very grave situation. Keep this forest of trees in mind. If any component has a 0 percent chance of achieving its goals, the product of all the components is necessarily 0.

This mathematics of uncertainty is as true of people as it is of components—team equaling software. Assuming that your team is appropriately load-balanced, that everybody is doing something critical, a single individual failure will naturally be a critical failure.

You will almost certainly never get either all of the components or all of the people to a 100 percent confidence level. In general, the odds are against success.

If one group are today's heroes, they will be tomorrow's villains. I continue to be amazed at the rapidity with which groups repeatedly rise to beatification and fall from grace. Make sure that you and the team understand this ultimate fragility of the enterprise and of reputations. That perspective will help contain bozo-bit flipping, arrogance, self-loathing, and the other evils born of frequent cycles of success and failure.

#47: *The world changes; so should you.*

One characteristic of excellence in software development is the capacity to make optimal decisions every day as new information becomes available. You don't want to be overcommitted to an artificial version of reality, which is what most plans and schedules really are. Change is pregnant with opportunity. If you are too committed to some course, that might make it difficult for you to adapt to the rapidly changing circumstances in which you find yourself. You might miss many of the most rewarding opportunities that present themselves. You'll perceive them as obstacles, as problems with the schedule or the plan, rather than as the creative opportunities they are.

There is a certain symmetry in the ongoing changes in a software development project. Often the failures and seemingly insurmountable difficulties facing the team are really an expression of the team's desire (or, to anthropomorphize, the project's desire) to go somewhere else. Before you go with a knee-jerk reaction, before you attack the problems head-on, take the time to analyze their geneses, theorize about their purposes, and try to use the forces that created them in an effort to exploit them. As in jujitsu. There are multiple meanings in every problem that manifests itself along the way. Use the richness of your native interpretive powers to determine the response (or the change) that is most in keeping with the natural flow of the development. Keep in mind that you are involved in a creative act of the group psyche. Its predictability will be inversely proportional to the degree of creativity.

Of course, you don't want to change plans willy-nilly. You are, after all, on a course and going in a direction. Excessive amounts of change result in thrashing and lack of progress. Flexibility is not the same thing as randomness. Flexibility is about reaching, stretching, and adapting in a natural progression, whereas randomness is about abrupt, discrete, unrelated changes. Randomness can be valuable when there is insufficient change, but insufficient change is seldom the problem. The changes you should accept or make are those that tend to optimize patterns already established, changes that move in the direction of simplicity and efficiency, not the ones that introduce new layers of complication.

Let's say, for example, that you contemplate adding a milestone to your schedule. No single indicator calls for this drastic change, but numerous harmonizing signs that the astute observer can perceive indicate that this is the direction the development "wants" to take. Perhaps certain launch opportunities combine with certain slippages and new feature opportunities along with excessive insecurity among the team about their dates—all of which combine to deliver a clear

Although you can summon the arguments for change, the courage doesn't necessarily follow.

message to anyone who cares to listen. I outline the coming together of such a particular set of circumstances because it happened on my team recently. Although we pride ourselves on shipping "on time," it became clear to us that we should take this heretical step, add a milestone to our schedule—basically flying in the face of accepted wisdom and all our previous experience. Like a child, each project is unique, with a life and personality of its own. You must validate the project's unique identity as you encounter signs of it and supply the particular project adequately for its journey. You have to relate to each project on its own terms, not according to some cookie-cutter process you've dreamed up or "learned."

Great software appears to have been created by a single great mind. It is inhabited by a single spirit. The extent to which your software exhibits this quality is related to your ability to guide the project through its many small, but momentous, changes. If you can identify and support the changes that best express the evolving spirit of the project, you'll preserve that spirit and make it available to your customers.

Resisting change is a losing strategy. Learn to identify irresistible and beneficial change, and then embrace it and adopt it. Make of such change your own, personal, change. In turn, the change will carry you to fruition. This difficult, scary undertaking calls for nerves of steel because you are relying on your discernment of things that others may not see. You might experience feelings of dissociation and loneliness, midnight tremors of doubt. Although you can summon the arguments for change, the courage doesn't necessarily follow. You'll be challenging people's expectations, and your own sense of self will change. You won't be convinced that it's a change for the good. You might be torn between accepting this new self and running, screaming, from the mirror.

Yet for all the angst, the destructive fury of change unheeded is incomparably worse. You'll find yourself opposing forces of immense power, and you'll surely be destroyed.

Even writing down thoughts such as these is frightening to me, but this is, in fact, what I experience in software development.

Ship
Mode

There is an ideal moment in every software development project when it's clearly time for the team to enter ship mode. Many people think of ship mode as the last headlong rush to get the product out the door. I prefer to identify stages in the ship mode period: *onset, transition,* and *endgame.* No, you can't cleanly differentiate among the stages: rather, in approximately the last third of the project you can see a progression of intensity and energy in which the three stages overlap and intermingle, primarily because different individuals on the team sequence through the stages at their own paces. But even with the blurring of precise distinctions, we can still see the gestalt.

Ship Mode: Onset

The onset of ship mode is gradual, like the onset of labor in childbirth. The team enters a preliminary kind of ship mode, a practice ship mode, toward the end of every milestone. If we were to extend the childbirth metaphor, we'd say that these early ship mode "contractions" are like Braxton-Hicks contractions. The organism is preparing for rather than entering into labor. And yes, it's fitting to refer to ship mode contractions. Completing the product calls for a contraction of focus and effort, a series of concentrated bursts of (usually) painful energy.

Let's assume we're talking about a four- or five-milestone project. Early milestones—M1, M2, and especially M3—will have at their ends certain ship mode characteristics. But as the project progresses and the ultimate goal of shipping gets within sight, the intensity of ship mode will be greatly magnified, its characteristics more pronounced. Genuine ship mode, the real thing, will commence toward the end of M3, typically, and will span the remaining one or two milestones in the project.

Often one of the first signs of the onset of ship mode is a conviction on the part of the more introspective team members that "we're not going to make it."

This judgment doesn't mean that the team and the project are not going to make it. It means that the best minds are starting to think through all the things that will have to happen before the product can ship. The sheer number of these activities will seem daunting, especially when only a few people so far are thinking about them. Fear or even panic might spread through the team like wildfire at the onset of ship mode as the people looking ahead and the project leaders take their fears public. By the time the panic has reached nearly everyone, the leaders will usually have calmed down because they've noted that everybody is now concerned about accomplishing the activities that will lead to shipment. This emotional jolt usually serves to increase the team's consciousness, its sense of togetherness, and its potential for greatness.

Some members of the team might think the leader is crazy.

The leader's role at this point is to take delight in the maturation of the project, to project confidence and enthusiasm in response to the team's increased awareness. Some members of the team might think the leader is crazy, but most of them will draw strength from the leader's proclaiming that this terror is a normal, expected, and acceptable response to the complexities and pressures of intellectual property creation.

The onset of ship mode initiates a high-performance period characterized by efficiency and determination. One hallmark of ship mode's onset is psychological and emotional closure on a variety of fronts.

❖ *The die is cast.* The product's features, the team, and their individual roles are solid. Up to this point, there has been a fair amount of "wobble": features have gone in and out and have been trimmed, there's been some load balancing, the architecture has been progressively refined, test plans and procedures have been evolving, documentation has been only outlined or sketched in, and many other aspects of the team's communal vision have been in the process of becoming more and more detailed and focused. Now there is little left to argue or wonder about. Everybody understands what the product is becoming. And they have a full awareness of what their remaining tasks are. Ship mode commences coincident with the team's awareness that the task is indeed finite. The only way out of the middle game and into ship mode is execution.

❖ *Nearly everybody believes.* Everybody (or nearly everybody) believes that achieving the next milestone and, ultimately, shipping the product, are possible in approximately the time allotted. All of the hard trade-offs have been made. There is a general consensus that the current course of action is the correct course. Ship mode marks the end of angst. Any paralyzing doubts are—if not eradicated—at least willingly suspended in favor of direct action. If there are serious unbelievers critical to the project— and what are they doing there at all if they aren't critical to the project?—

ship mode has not and will not commence until their doubts have been resolved.

❖ *Nearly everybody understands.* Things are concrete enough that understanding is widespread. All members of the team understand precisely what they need to do to get the product to ship. Most if not all unknowns have been factored out. Contingency plans are in place for those few obstinate unknowns that haven't yet yielded to the drive for certainty. Lateness and the fear of lateness are now directly related to the tasks at hand. They're no longer the generalized worry, the free-floating anxiety, that had earlier preoccupied the team. I sometimes think of ship mode as list mode: at the commencement of ship mode, every single team member should basically have a list of things to do, a plan for how and when to do them, and a time for when each will be done. When all of the items on all of the lists are done, the product ships.

The top leaders of the team must lead the team through ship mode by entering ship mode first and sustaining their commitment to it throughout. Their awareness of detail climbs, they eliminate superfluous management hoo-ha—fire drills and other de-prioritizing activities—entirely, and they bring tremendous focus to bear on shipping. Management at this point is interested only in talking about completing the product, in what steps will get us there most quickly. At this stage, leaders should fan the team's desire to ship. Generally, their having given the team a complete awareness of the effect of shipping (or not shipping) will have created the desire.

Ship Mode: Transition

The transitional stage of ship mode can span one or more milestones, so you need to pace yourself and the team. The transition in this stage of ship mode is basically from implementation to endgame stabilization. Implementation is still going on, generally, until the final milestone. And the product keeps destabilizing under the influence of this implementation effort. Naturally, this reduces the intensity of ship mode. It can be exhausting to keep forcing the product into some kind of stable state so that ship mode can resume with greater force. During the transitional phase, people will increasingly feel that bug fixing should be the only activity going on, that whatever features remain unimplemented should be abandoned. Although there will be pressure in this direction, generally, this is a type of panic response, expressing more emotion than product development sensibility. You need to exhaustively analyze each troubling feature before you abandon it.

Look at ship mode as a continuum of increasing focus. As ship mode progresses and implementation slows, the team enters into the "endgame." (See the next page.) Look for and encourage transitional and early endgame signs.

❖ The team become especially vigilant about thinking things through and about looking for traps.

❖ The team make check-ins with extra precautions. Often an *ad hoc* team of peers review the code before it's checked in.

❖ Performance tuning and UI tweaks get more emphasis; polishing the product, fit, and finish become the significant issues.

❖ As the fine-tuning is accomplished, stabilization of the product increasingly becomes the principal goal. All development but for bug fixing is nearing completion.

Ship Mode: Endgame

As the transition from the onset of ship mode to the endgame nears completion, the team's focus will shift. In the endgame, there is only one more milestone: shipping. Conceptually, the endgame is a very simple exercise. The team maintain a list of activities. When every activity on the list is complete, you ship. The list might contain hundreds or thousands of items, but it's still just a list. There's no time for any effort that doesn't contribute to completing the items on the list. Every person on the team is expected to complete his or her items as promised. As unanticipated items arise, after appropriate resistance, they are put on the list. The appropriate level of resistance is *profound resistance*.

It's a good idea to establish a daily meeting, with the final decision-makers in attendance. The agenda should be *ad hoc*, assembled at the beginning of each meeting. No item that can be handled immediately should be postponed. The team should know that all issues can be brought to this meeting for expeditious remedy. Management is involved, leading the team toward their goal. The goal now is an acceptable level of quality at ship time. This is the bug fix stage, but only showstopper bugs should be addressed, the bugs that will either affect more than a handful of users or cause unacceptably serious errors. Cosmetic changes, performance enhancements, new functions are

How many low-priority bugs did your product ship with last time?

not appropriate in the endgame. Beta feedback at this stage is to affirm that there are no showstoppers, provide advance warning of unanticipated market reaction, and provide input for the next release.

You need to know the range of quality that's acceptable to your customers. How many low-priority bugs did your product ship with last time? Was it a problem? With respect to a particular bug, ask, Are the customers better off with this product, including this bug? Since destabilizing the software will create more of a problem than most bugs will, be very careful about which bugs you fix. The ones you choose not to fix are why products ship with readme's and bug lists.

Sometimes, just as labor can falter or even stop for long periods of time before childbirth, so too the ship mode process can totter or even collapse on the way to shipping. The following rules of thumb can provide some guidance to the team and its leadership on initiating and sustaining ship mode until the spanking-new product arrives.

#48: *Violate at least one sacred cow.*

You may be tempted to try, but you can't make people work as hard as they will have to. There's no way to mandate the kind of fervor and sacrifice that will be required of the team to meet the hellish challenge of ship mode. I've seen clueless managers who didn't have a good understanding of human motivation try the heavy-handed approach, try to coerce people into working evenings and weekends. The response I've usually observed is the equivalent of the whole team's collectively flipping the bird at their pathetic manager.

But the leader's role doesn't disappear during ship mode. Symbolic actions, for instance, count tremendously. The effective manager or leader will make a grand symbolic gesture that says that the team and their commitments to each other are more important than anything else in the company or the business unit. Such a gesture will pay enormous dividends in intensifying the concentrated effort in ship mode.

The symbolic communication should be motivational—providing free lattes, having a masseur walk the halls giving people brief massages, providing for weekend childcare (insurance be damned), supplying food to the team (preferably out of your own pocket), making special arrangements for people to work at home, and so on. The point here is that such gestures be particularly solicitous and, ideally, against the rules. By winking at the rules, you tell the team that their well-being and their ability to reach their goals are values you hold higher than any other. And the psychology of developers is such that they love to rebel against authority and structure, a trait that in other circumstances produces the piratical hacker mentality.

Developers love to rebel against authority and structure.

Take symbolic actions that also show the team that this ship mode experience, though (ideally) short-lived, nevertheless has historical significance. Take their pictures, tell tales of other ship mode experiences, create legends and mythology, send e-mail that congratulates exemplary and, preferably, humorous examples of outstanding ship mode behavior.

Enjoy this time, and your joy will be contagious. Ship mode is the climax of the teambuilding experience. As the team come together in a miraculous burst of creative energy, all divisiveness and foolishness are left behind. When the teamwork is done, the product ships.

#49: *Beta is not the time to change.* _____

There is a nearly universal misconception that Beta testing is for soliciting input on the design and implementation of the features in the product. Nothing could be further from the truth. Betas are to ensure that the product works as expected in as wide a variety of machine configurations as possible. Although opinions from Beta testers are always interesting, unless the feedback is overwhelmingly calamitous, no genuine changes except those that fix configuration problems are warranted. Other feedback and ideas go onto the list for the next revision.

Don't confuse this view of the Beta process with a disregard for customer input. On the contrary, if you've waited until Beta stage to solicit customer input, you'll never ship. Your relationship with the customer should have been much more intimate and ongoing. (See the discussion "The Customer" in the "Opening Moves" section of this book.)

#50: *The Beta is for spin development.* _____

Customers' first impressions are the raw material of *spin*. What the Beta testers first see and feel is what everyone will first see and feel. It's the marketer's job to capitalize on those perceptions and emotions by playing off against them in the product's messages. Even though at that stage the core messages may well be cast in unalterable media, the sensitive marketer will engage intensively with Beta customers. There will still be opportunity to add and soften emphases based on Beta response. The marketer should create a model of the emotional state of the customer as he or she uses the product. That's the model that should be in the minds of those who craft messages about the product.

Undoubtedly, inevitably, you'll receive some negative reaction to some aspects of your new product. This is normal and only to be expected. If the negative responses are consistent in type and severity, you have an opportunity to develop a more balanced spin on your product. If it seems that everyone is going to have a particular negative response, it's best to anticipate that and set expectations so that the negative response will be unsurprising. This feat of anticipation alone should reduce the negative response by orders of magnitude.

The marketing people should be deeply engaged in, if not driving, the Beta process. At this stage of the game, communications about the product are infinitely more malleable than the product itself. Restrict your development efforts to the development of messages.

#51: *Triage ruthlessly.* _____

If your software is a pure expression of your team, it will have near-limitless imperfections. This lack of perfection is in the nature of intellectual property creation. For that matter, it's in the nature of everything: I defy you to show me a

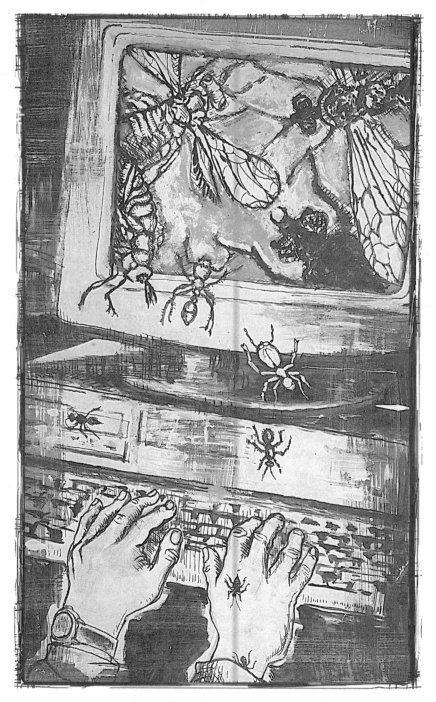

Bugs

perfect *anything*. The question is not how perfect the software is; rather, it's how good the judgment of the team is in determining which imperfections to remediate. We call the process of developing and applying this judgment "triage."

"Triage," of course, is derived from emergency medicine, in which all incoming cases are rapidly evaluated with an eye toward selecting the most critical cases for prioritized treatment. Software triage is a similar analysis of incoming bugs and other defects. There are several dimensions to triaging bugs during ship mode (or at any other time, for that matter).

❖ *The severity of the bug.* A pertinent question to ask, especially in the endgame, is whether you would recall the product if this bug were discovered after the product had shipped. Is it a showstopper?

❖ *Significance.* Would a defect of this type be perceived as symbolic of a more general quality problem? Would this be an embarrassing bug?

❖ *Extent.* What percentage of your customers will encounter this bug?

❖ *The potential for destabilizing the software by remediating the bug.* This call requires an acute eye, an understanding of the software architecture and its flaws, and excellent judgment about the risk-appropriateness of the proposed fix.

❖ *Team dynamics.* Would the bug have to be resolved by a group or a person already overwhelmed or otherwise ill-equipped to deal with it?

❖ *The extent to which regression testing resources will be required to validate the fix.* Are there enough resources? Is there enough time?

In general, the triage team is trying to shape a product that, defects and all, will have overwhelmingly clear benefit to the majority of the customers the majority of the time. Will they be better off with or without this imperfect product? To develop this sophisticated triage esthetic requires that the team be attuned to the customers and one another and that they be reciprocally skilled.

#52: *Don't shake the Jell-O.*

Develop in your team a horror of changing the product. You have to get to ship quality for only one moment, but you have to coerce that moment into being. You do that by focusing all of your energy on stabilization, on reducing the rate and the number of bug fixes and eliminating regressions.

Shipping a product is like watching a large-sized serving of quivering Jell-O. Gradually, the Jell-O slows its vibrations. But then you fix a bunch of bugs, and it starts quivering frenetically again. Then slowly, ever so slowly, the quivering subsides. You wait, focused and primed, for the instant the Jell-O stops shaking. Then…you ship it!

And then it starts shaking again.

The
Launch

While *Dynamics of Software Development* is primarily about the core activity of producing great software with a development team, I would be remiss if I didn't address the essential, inseparable role of communications in the production and dissemination of great software. Greatness in anything, after all, is difficult for most of us to perceive because by its nature greatness involves something new or transcendent. To my mind, this novelty means that greatness, in addition to being integral to the software itself, must be communicated. Because greatness has to do with historicity, we can appreciate it most readily in historical terms.

Launch is the moment your product enters history. Your customers and critics commence at this moment to determine what it is and what it means. Even if you don't produce commercial, shrink-wrapped software, you should develop an understanding of the role of launches and apply launch techniques to your situation. There is always some forum or gathering, or you can create one, at which you can launch

A launch event is a supercharged manifestation of success.

your new technology. It's essential that your product have a debut or premiere and that you broadcast its messages in all situations. The fanfare and the communication are important parts of your relationship with your customers and with the product team. The launch is the primary event within and around which expectations are set and motivations and personality are made manifest.

Launches are not retractable. A message can of course be recast, but the usual result of revision is not the pervasiveness of the new, recast message; usually the result is simply confusion. In a properly planned and implemented launch, all relevant sensibilities are focused on the product. You have people's attention. Putting out a crystal clear message supported by a gleaming new product and excellent communications materials will pay enormous dividends. The benefits of an effective launch are practically immeasurable:

❖ *A specific launch event with a fixed date will focus the team.* If something has to happen by a certain date, it often will. A product development team responds well to the challenge of providing the product at an opportune moment. I suggest that all parties who have a role in the activities leading up to, including, and following the launch have their own war room. The launch of a product is a campaign, in many ways a product of its own. All of the teamwork requirements discussed at length in this book apply to the launch team as well. There must be vision, strategy, and tactics. There must be a commitment to high-quality execution. The entire team will find it enjoyable to succeed, and a launch event, with product in hand, is a supercharged manifestation of success. The current of successful energy will infect all who participate in the launch.

❖ *A launch event can put emotion into the reception of the product.* The key influencers who will lead opinion about your product are especially susceptible to such an event. A launch event is an opportunity for drama. Most people who attend a launch event are there for sheer love of the business or the technology, or because of the personal impact of your software on their lives. Their emotions are available. They are inclined to identify with you, your effort, your feelings, and your product. They know you through their use of your products. Be sure the feelings you express and the symbols you manipulate are the most powerful and meaningful you can summon. Work with marketers who understand both the historical and the technological significance of what you've achieved as well as how to exploit its dramatic potential.

❖ *A launch event is the centerpiece of an orchestrated rollout.* The activities leading up to the launch event and those that follow it need to be scheduled in a logical sequence. The press, key customers, influencers, and friends should have been in the Beta program, of course, so that they'll be familar with the product and be willing to serve as references. Before launch, they should be briefed privately. They will thus be primed, ready to break with the news or endorsements at the moment of launch. At the moment of launch, all the communications materials break: ads, datasheets, mailers, point-of-sale exhibits—whatever is appropriate. You follow this up with innovative customer support and expeditious servicing of demand. All of these details, the whole rollout, carry your messages. No matter the scale of the effort, or even the degree of privacy if you are servicing internal clients, you can and should bring all of these elements to bear on your product's rollout.

#53: *Compete with the superior story.*

In every great software product is a great story. (Mediocre products have mediocre stories.) Messages have an architecture every bit as complex as the software itself. Messages must transmit on multiple levels. They must resonate emotionally and cognitively with their recipients. They must evolve and build over time. They must be simple enough to have high communications value yet complex enough to retain interest and provide challenging overtones and undertones. Obviously, the quality of your message architecture will have a great deal to do with the success of your product. Be sure you have invested as appropriately in your message development as you have in your product development. In the final analysis, messages are inseparable from their products. All are intellectual property created by the team.

Conventional wisdom gets repeated endlessly without your further ministrations.

Understand the architecture of your communications strategy. How will what be transmitted? How will you get people to think what you know they need to think before they can appreciate your product? Your messages are the light that makes your product visible.

When you sit down with your key audiences, don't simply launch into demos and features. Give your product some context. Your account of this context is the story you'll tell to a variety of audiences: the team, management, the press, analysts, customers, investors—whoever has an interest in your product, market, business, or technology. Design the story so that it becomes conventional wisdom. Conventional wisdom will be repeated endlessly without your further ministrations. And conventional wisdom in any field has some common characteristics.

Conventional wisdom is based on simple insight. Your story has to have at least one element (and no more than three) that is an insight into market conditions or technology trends or both. This insight is the reason people will listen to the story, the value they gain from it. The insight should be simple, however, because influencers are less likely to listen to (and will have a harder time repeating) too-subtle perceptions. To qualify as an insight, the perception should have original elements. If it doesn't, it will evoke the jaded response we all have to older insights that have devolved into cliches. And in order to be a *simple* insight, the perception has to be one that any creative and knowledgeable person who gave the matter much thought and had a certain amount of courage might have on his or her own. Don't confuse *simple* with *simplistic*, though. Oversimplified concepts tend to be demagogic, not insightful. It's essential that your insight be of value to the listener.

You want to get the listener to say, "That's just what I was thinking!"

The Software Story

Creating this insightful little packet of information can be quite challenging, like creating a well-turned haiku. The goal is to articulate an insight that gives coherence and validity to the inchoate thoughts and feelings of the listener. You want to get the listener to say, "That's what I was thinking!" You're shooting for the insight born of common sense, meant to inform and shape opinion, not straining to impress. The insight must be the kind of thing that, once spoken, everybody thinks was always known to be true.

Often developing such an insight will mean taking a slightly different tack with unacknowledged but widely perceived facts: "The reason customers don't use foobars is that foobars are just too hard to use!" The insight should be as iconoclastic as pointing out that the emperor is wearing no clothes—but not too radical. Take one "fact" that you're convinced people believe or would believe (but that no one has expressed), and tie it to another fact (step two) that leads to your product. Don't ever express something that somebody else's campaign has already expressed.

When we launched Visual C++ 1.0 (upon which we had banked everything), for example, the fact we selected to emphasize was that most C programmers had not yet moved from C to C++. We had data that suggested that while over 80 percent of C programmers wanted to, planned to, or hoped to move to C++ in the near future, only 10 percent had actually been able to make the move. The press and analysts thought that the C++ revolution had already happened.

It's more effective not to say the most important thing.

Our data showed otherwise, and we said so. This was our way of saying that the emperor had no clothes.

We had no difficulty persuading people of our fact because it was true and it squared with our audience's sense of reality. Any outfit would have uncovered the same basic fact eventually, had they taken the time and the trouble.

Step two in creating our story was to tie the fact to our product. This was simple: C++ was too hard to use even for C programmers—before Visual C++. What made it too hard? All the things that Visual C++ made easy.

Conventional wisdom can be expressed in a sizzler. A sizzler is a "sound bite," a one- or two-sentence summation or symbolic representation of the insight that is memorable and repeatable. Political campaigns are great at coming up with sizzlers: "What this country needs is a good 5 cent cigar." "We have nothing to fear but fear itself." "Ask not what your country can do for you, but what you can do for your country." Conventional wisdom becomes conventional because it provides accessible guidance to people who have neither the time nor the inclination to master complex topics. It survives as long as it provides productive guidance for the people who depend on it. But if they can't access the wisdom, it will wither and die, so expressing the insight with a memorable sizzler is key.

A good story enables people who espouse it to feel clever. Once they grasp your insight (which they will do because it's simple), people can readily adopt it as their own. They will tend to do that in proportion to the degree of insightfulness your sizzler confers on them, its utility to them, its memorability, and its malleability—they will want to tweak it to make it their own. It was conventional wisdom of a particular football coach, for example, that "he always loses the big ones." People

You want those brains to connect new synapses on their own as they bank your insight.

would tweak that to "he's no good in the clutch," or "he would be a great coach if he didn't always lose the big ones." The point is to provide an insight that people can work over and put into their own language.

If you can provide your story with the classic elements of good storytelling—mood, plot, good guys, bad guys, excitement, and chase scenes—so much the better. Make it vivid by emphasizing the human and emotional dimension of the story. Have your best storyteller create it and teach others to tell it.

A good story is supported by solid evidence. Usually, though, people use way too much evidence. Their point gets lost in all the noise. One or two key facts will do it, no more than three. Give them something they'll remember because of its significance and its simplicity. Just make sure your facts clearly support, or better, even tell, the story.

The story has to support repetition by all the key people on your team, and, more important, by the people you hope will retell it spontaneously as it transmogrifies into conventional wisdom. With a couple of key facts, some feelings, and a human angle, the story will be crisp and memorable.

Interestingly, it is much more effective not to say the most important thing. What you want to do instead is make the most important thing an unmistakable conclusion the listener will draw. For example, when we launched Visual C++ 1.0, the most important thing to us was that the press, analysts, and the market understand that Microsoft was back in the C++ business with a vengeance, that we had turned around, that we were now the leader, the one to catch. We never said any of that in our story. It's simply not credible (or attractive) to pound your chest and proclaim your greatness. Instead, you must make the ultimate message come together in the minds of your audience. Present your audience with a rich subtext to your story that will lead them to the conclusion you want them to reach. Your audience's brains are your ultimate medium. You want those brains to connect new synapses on their own as they bank your insight. The messages really come together most effectively only when that happens.

#54: *Create a winning image.*

To underlie all of your efforts, products, and messages, you must create a winning image, for several reasons.

❖ *Customers identify with their software.* Software is one of those things, like cars or homes, with which customers strongly identify. Probably because they spend so much time using their software, they tend to view themselves as a *product x* expert, or a *product y* user. Even the terminology is suggestive: customers don't *buy* software; they *adopt* it. Think about that.

❖ *Customers want something others perceive as desirable.* The software they use is a measure of your customers' status, their "with-it-ness." As they see it, their relevance in this computer era is determined in large measure by your relevance. The latest software is the best, the most fashionable. Fashion is a powerful motivator. If you think you should dismiss fashion as superfluous in purchasing decisions, consider your tie purchases or car purchases or hemline consciousness. (Also see Rule #14: "Take the oxygen along.")

❖ *Customers know that they're in a software relationship, not a one-shot affair.* They're buying into a relationship with you, not merely buying a product. They will be buying many releases over long stretches of time, and their expertise will become more and more narrowly focused on your technology. They don't want to be connected with a loser: that would make them losers.

All of your communications efforts must portray you as a desirable, winning group. Remember, though, that winners don't talk about winning. They just win.

The Last Word

If I had to come up with one conclusive thought, it would be, Development develops developers.

But the really appropriate last word comes from the classic ending of Roman Polanski's *Chinatown*. Jake, the Jack Nicholson character, is baffled and upset over the psychological and emotional enormities he's just undergone. His sidekick rallies Jake with a summing up of the entire experience. "C'mon, Jake," he says, "it's Chinatown."

Of course, there is no last word on software development. You have to go back to the beginning of the book (and of the game) and start all over on the next level.

But remember, Jake, it's software . . .

Appendix:

Hiring and Keeping Good People

You want to hire the best people you can find, and you want to take good care of them so that they'll give you their most effective work and stay around to build a dynamic team capable of the revolutionary growth the software development industry routinely demands of its players.

This much is obvious. How to do it in a software development environment, however, is a bit of a specialty.

Hiring Smart

Finding smart people to hire is difficult, but it's worth doing because smart people tend to survive. In a software career, an individual has to cope with many negative experiences: inept bosses, bad design choices, work on the wrong product, dysfunctional teams, wildly late projects. These are challenging but normal software development experiences, and being smart is the most useful attribute a team member can have if he or she is to transcend such difficulties and emerge with a truly effective career. And of course, software is intellectual property, so you want to get as much intellect for your buck as you can.

As you interview to hire smart, look for a number of key characteristics and interview events.

Look for the ineffable spark of intelligence. There are as many ways of expressing intelligence as there are individuals who possess it. It is the nature of intelligence to be idiosyncratic, and this uniqueness is the key to finding smart people for your team. Look for individuation, the most visible manifestation of intelligence.

Check out the candidate's affect. What does the way the candidate presents his or her personality say? Choices are being made. What do the choices signify? Watch the play of emotion and intellect on the candidate's face. Is anybody home? Ideally, you'll detect that there's *much* more going on than is superficially apparent.

You have to slow down a bit and analyze things to determine how deep the person is, how much potential the person has.

Gauge your own emotional and intellectual responses to the candidate. Does the candidate challenge you to think more deeply, probe more subtly, assess more rapidly? Does the candidate draw out the best you have to offer? How does the whole encounter feel? Are you learning anything about anything?

Interviews are basically scripts, the roles predetermined and somewhat rigid. Does the candidate respond as expected? Are you surprised by anything the candidate says, or by the way he or she says it? Does the candidate break out of the formulaic role spontaneously? Can you nudge the candidate out of the role? Does the candidate seem to be flexible? Does he or she have an appropriate appetite for information—and the security to go after it? If the candidate is smart, his or her intelligence will probably have an impact on you and on the evolution of the interview itself. If the candidate can influence the course of the interview, it's likely that he or she can influence the course of other, more complicated, events.

Challenge the candidate with a puzzle. Your posing a real-world problem can elicit a lot of information about the candidate. Almost all candidates will assume that they are being tested. And they are, but not only in the dimensions of which they are aware. Naturally, you want the candidate to demonstrate that he or she will take reasonable approaches to solving the problem you pose, but more interesting are the observations you can make and the inferences you can draw about the candidate's working style.

Does the candidate quickly make erroneous assumptions about the problem? Almost everyone does, at least initially. Or does the candidate go to work on a clarification of the problem, soliciting more and more information until the problem domain has been clearly defined and how an answer might look has been fully envisioned? On several occasions, I've asked people how they would do something when it was clear to me that they wouldn't know how to do it and it was equally clear to them that I did. Rather than try to prove themselves, the smartest candidates will simply ask me how to do the task. Of course, most of us are too stubborn, too defensive, and just generally too unwise to simply ask for help.

See what happens if you volunteer help. Candidates respond to an offer of help in an interview situation in an infinite variety of interesting ways. I respect someone who first asks whether the acceptance of help will be considered a sign of weakness.

Try teaching. Assert your expertise, and see what happens. Does the candidate absorb what you have to offer? Ask for more information? Elaborate on your teaching? Apply it? Resist it? Does the candidate have a better idea?

Keep in mind that your goal is to hire people to whom you can grant a considerable amount of responsibility, people you will entrust with the future of your product and empower to manage your technology. A candidate's relationship to authority figures—to you in the interview situation—will be a key determinant of his or her future performance. You want to find out whether the candidate can set ego aside in order to solve a problem or learn something.

Take off the blinders. The biggest mistake I see managers make as they hire people for software development teams is that they overvalue a particular technical skill. To verify this tendency, all you have to do is look at the want ads: "Wanted: foobar programmers. Experience with whatsit required." Obviously, conversance with a given technology is a wonderful attribute in a candidate, but in the final analysis it's an extra, not a mandatory. After all, most software development technologies have a half-life of about one year. Much more important than a particular technical skill is a *history* of relevant skills accumulation. I want to see the trajectory of a candidate's career: What skills were acquired when? Does the candidate's history show an ability to focus on key technologies at the right moment in time?

Giving Good People Someplace to Go

If you've hired smart, you want to benefit from your perspicacity for a good long time to come. You won't profit much from your discernment of potential if you don't help individual team members and the team as a whole to realize their gifts. At any given moment, your team will probably be made up of what I call racehorses and overreachers. The same team member might fall into each of these categories at different times and several times. As their manager, your obligation is to figure out what's going on in your team's careers and in your team's career and to reconcile the two.

Racehorses Have to Run

A team member can be so successful, grow so significantly, that he or she obviously needs greater range to sustain that rate of growth. Management's job is to recognize the successful individual's transcendence of his or her current role and provide more room. If management is blind to the situation or delays, prevaricates, or otherwise endeavors to dawdle over the problem, the successful individual will inevitably begin to prey on weaker members of the team or wander off looking for greener pastures. Healthy team members won't starve themselves.

As my Iowan father used to say, "When there isn't enough feed in the feedlot, the pigs'll eat each other."

Anyone is either growing or withering away. Staying the same is not an option. If you are shipping more frequently, increasing sales, increasing market share, increasing customer satisfaction, or seeing virtually anything that indicates positive change in results, your team is growing. Otherwise, it's not.

The challenges your team faces must grow in proportion to the growth of the individual team members, in lockstep with their growth, really. Often the first sign that the team's challenges aren't keeping up with the growth of individuals is that those most rapidly growing team members have become restless. Complaints about the general environment have increased. The big victories seem to be behind you. People have started to talk about the good old days, and they may have begun to look around. This dissatisfaction and restlessness signify that you aren't providing sufficient challenge to the team.

Now is the time to change. Take some big risks. Find out what key individuals want to do, what they would find challenging. You've empowered them. Now get them to question the destiny of your business and its relationship to their personal destinies. What kind of environment do they want to create? What sorts of products do they dream of building? Find the fit.

Grow. Make new investments. Try wholly new things. Have people utterly change roles. Don't hesitate. Everybody must grow, from the highest leader to the front ranks. Growth is inevitable, and you must find an outlet for it.

The Problem of Creativity

Creativity in a group is always limited by the group's defensiveness, and some amount of defensiveness is healthy. In the healthy team, then, no matter how highly valued creativity is ostensibly, change beyond a certain normative quantity or degree will be resisted. And even change within bounds will be accepted only insofar as it can seem to fall under the rubric of "improvement." Change must seem to build on the previously known and accepted reality. Even if there are only two steps involved in a change, with the second building on the first, in a single reality cycle—a single product development cycle for us—the change is likely to be rejected by the healthy team.

What you need for truly creative change, then, is an environment that transcends good health, an environment that not only accepts a continuum of change, which is normal, but one that positively engenders, nurtures, and propels forward wholly new dynamics. The transcendent organization values radical or revolutionary change and esteems utterly new modes of thought. It's possible for a team to be healthy and not especially creative, but this state of affairs is not especially desirable. What is desirable is team fecundity, the radiating of the new and the original from the normal and the healthy.

(continued)

This kind of creativity requires a flexibility and a courage beyond the reach of most of us most of the time.

It's ironic and worth remembering that the healthier the team the more effective the resistance to revolutionary thought will be. This is a natural consequence of the team's overall effectiveness in every relevant domain.

Overreachers Need a Boost

Sometimes an individual team member will have a role appetite greater than his or her digestive capacity. This appetite might stem from a much earlier and more fundamental psychological "appetite" that was left unsatisfied. The fundamental historical dissatisfaction is carried forward and transferred to the current team situation. We might call the result pathological ambition: the desire for greater range when the current range is abundant. The reward of additional range comes naturally to the team member who needs it to avoid starving. The pathologically ambitious are hungry beyond their needs, and their appetites will probably never be sated. Appropriately sensing the potential for waste, the rest of the team won't support their acquisition of additional range.

It's also normal in the early maturation of a gifted team member that he or she masters a narrow field but doesn't yet understand that it is a narrow field. In such a period, the team member tends to blame the poor judgment of management for his or her inability to grow beyond that narrow field of vision and ultimately has his or her naive ideals brutally shattered. If the team member's career is managed well, he or she will leave this period more effective by an order of magnitude. But too many employees get stuck in this period and end up embittered, prematurely leveled people, stunted people. You need to know how to bring a team member through this dangerous period successfully, that is, for the benefit of the individual and of the team.

Grok the goals. Make sure you fully understand what a team member who seems to be overreaching wants to do. You'll usually uncover some indecision or an overly ambitious goal related to a position that currently exists, usually higher up in the hierarchy. The indecision (which usually takes the form of mutually contradictory goals) or the ambitious goal the team member expresses at first is important because it is the foundation for your work together.

Most likely, the overreacher's goal represents some role or value especially symbolic to him, something other than its literal expression. Try to understand what it represents or symbolizes. Ask some good questions: What does this goal mean to you? How appropriate is it? How likely do you think you are to reach it? If you were to reach this goal, what would you want to use it for? And check out your own feelings: How do I feel about this goal? For the other person? For anyone else on the team? For myself?

Reconcile the models. Once you and the team member are certain you understand what the goal actually is, you need to decide whether the goal is consistent with his capabilities and with the team vision. If the goal is beyond the team member's reach, find out why. There is meaning in the disconnection. How did such a self-misperception arise? Deal with this issue candidly and exhaustively and over a long period of time. The team member will of course be extremely sensitive over what he perceives to be a negative judgment about his potential or his choice of a career course. It will take some time for him to believe that you're an ally who genuinely understands and supports his ambition to grow.

Make sure you understand his personal theory of management or software development; that is, get some insight into what he's *trying* to do. Neither he nor you may realize that he has a theory or a collection of underlying, unstated assumptions and articles of belief about the team's undertaking. You must ferret out his assumptions. Once you feel confident that you understand his view of what the team is supposed to be up to (and this may take a surprising amount of non-judgmental, value-free inquiry), assess the ambition vis-à-vis your team's effort. Is his model consistent with your own and with what you understand of the rest of the team's vision and values? Does his ambition support what the team is trying to create?

Your job, finally, is to devise ways and solicit help to align his goals with his capabilities and with the team's vision.

Find the genius. Now that you understand what he wants and his theory of operation, set it all aside for the moment and work to identify the one to three things he does better than anyone else, the things which, if they were all he needed to do, would make him the most wildly successful person in history! Have a dialogue with the team member about these perceptions of yours. If he agrees, begin to shape his assignment so that the things he excels at are all or most of what is expected from him.

In theory, at least, this shouldn't be hard. It is (almost) always easier to play to someone's strengths than to remedy his deficiencies. But you'll need courage to throw out some of your assumptions about the job categories you're filling. It takes an insightful and brave manager—having failed at this a number of times, I feel eminently qualified to say what kind of manager it takes—to reshape the organization so that the individual genius of each person can shine forth.

New Categories

As I write, I have been mentoring a gifted woman in our group. Her five years' experience consisted of successful program management, primarily in another group, so we in our group had had little direct experience of her conventional program management skills. Her expressed goal was to become a manager at a higher level; that is, she wanted to manage people for a living.

As the rest of the team and I grew to know this team member, we saw that she did in fact have an uncanny ability to diagnose interpersonal situations—team conflicts and a variety of dysfunctionalities—and to suggest good ways to straighten out professional relationships. In other words, she was a killer group diagnostician with a genius for empathy and analysis. More and more people sought her out for advice and guidance in complex situations. This happened naturally, with the least amount of encouragement from me.

The more I thought about it and discussed it with her, the more I realized that the maintenance of a healthy team required the ongoing insight and support and, frequently, the direct intervention of someone with her skill set. It looked like an investment that would pay back dozens of times in reduced friction, cleaner professional interactions, and increased productivity. Supervision is an outmoded concept. She didn't really have to "supervise" people in order to apply her genius. She just needed the support of the team and its leadership to perform this role.

Although we haven't figured out all of the details yet, she and I have become convinced that we should create a new category of team member. We haven't decided what the title should be, but the function will be "effectiveness analysis and remediation." She will consult with people and pitch in on feature teams where ineffective behavior is a noticeable problem. We have decided that she should pioneer this role, document it, develop the principles of the office, develop the training and career path for it, and generally exercise the role to the extent that our results warrant it.

It can pay huge dividends to rethink things anew. Innovation starts with you.

As you work to uncover and encourage the genius in your team members, remember that people are often most tentative about their highest gifts. I know I am, at any rate, and several people I work closely with are as well. I think this is because our sublimest gifts are the aspects of ourselves we most highly prize, the things that most individuate and personalize us. We hold very dear the idea that we are special because of these gifts, and we are wary of putting these nourishing self-assessments to the test. Expressing our gifts in a possibly judgmental forum is a high-risk deal.

The Manager Managed

Just a short time ago my boss, Denis Gilbert, helped me identify a significant personal block. Over the years I have developed a freewheeling talk on software development practices that I give several times a year at various forums all over the world. People rave about it, and I enjoy doing it immensely, both because of the affirmation I get and because I feel like I'm giving something back. (This talk, by the way, is the father of this book.)

Denis knew that I was having success with my talk, that I was using it to help software development professionals everywhere—everywhere, that is, except at Microsoft! I was afraid to give my talk at home. Sure, anyone could have argued—and I knew—that there were bound to be groups at Microsoft that could have benefited from hearing my talk. But my fear of rejection, my respect (overawe?) for my colleagues, and my unwillingness to risk presenting my gifts where I had made my biggest professional commitment had paralyzed me.

Once Denis called out this singularity and simultaneously affirmed that I was good at this kind of speaking and that many people (even at Microsoft!) could profit from hearing about my experiences in software development, I felt sufficiently enabled to offer the talk to anyone who cared to listen, even at Microsoft, and at the drop of a hat. (Of course, now Denis probably regrets creating a Frankenstein monster: here I sit writing a book on the subject while Visual C++ goes untended.)

Some self-destructive or fearful tendency creates the block. It comes from within the person, not from the rest of the world. In a properly empowered environment, it's not within management's capability to block people; it's within management's power only to help people unblock themselves.

People are just naturally hypersensitive about their gifts, but if you in your capacity as the authority figure validate them and give them permission, they'll grow exponentially in the direction in which they're prone to grow. You have to constantly encourage them, challenge them to do what they're good at, support them in appropriate risk-taking, and praise them for doing well and taking risks.

They'll tend to discount their own potential at first. It's your job to tell them they're a genius at this one thing, that they can do it, that you are counting on them to do it, that it's essential that they do it, and so on. You need to tell them in countless ways that nothing else matters in comparison to the use of their gifts.

I can think of several cases in which uncovering, validating, and then empowering the genius in someone has paid off handsomely. People are usually surprised when you notice how good they are at something, and then they increase their efforts in the identified direction exponentially. Since they're doing what they're naturally good at, their effectiveness soars. And significant reciprocal loyalty develops in tandem with a cycle of mutual achievement and respect.

To be understood, effective, and appreciated is the highest reward of professional life.

Find ways to communicate these emotionally difficult ideas. Such discussions are both challenging and crucial, and they often cause managers to give off a weird affect. So do your homework. Spend two hours in preparation for every half-hour meeting. Craft your message carefully. Develop a strategy for getting your message across. Then make sure you got it across.

Don't try to cover too many ideas at once. Make each vivid. Be sure that you apply your own unique gifts to the job at hand. Take yourself and your charge seriously. In some ways, both of your lives do depend on it.

Be reassuring. Work at it with the person you're helping until you're sure that the fundamental idea has detached from your ego and become available to the team member.

Get help. Make use of other people's gifts as you work on this problem. Along with your own skills and intelligence, there are most likely many incredibly talented individuals you can access for advice and support. Don't be dumb; ask for help. The main thing to remember is that you are not alone and that you probably have the richest supply of skills imaginable at your beck and call. Don't go it alone. Don't be afraid to express vulnerability by asking for help. Vulnerability is one of the most attractive human traits and can inspire a great deal of loyalty.

Set short-term expectations. Decide with the team member what near-term behavior will demonstrate progress. Make the clock on this behavior goal extra-short (days, not weeks; weeks, not months). Look your mentee right in the eye, and tell him that you're giving him your very best and that you expect him to reciprocate. If he shows by his behavior that he prefers not to reciprocate, close down the discussion. You've told him up front that reciprocity is the basis of the deal: you give your best only to a team member who wants to act on it. You've provided an opportunity, a chance to gain from having encountered you. He can take it or not. If he doesn't, you proceed to the next most likely candidate.

Have a long-term theory. Know what a fully realized person in the new category, with this constellation of gifts, would look like over the long haul. Know where he is on the time continuum at all moments. Catch setbacks. Define "normal" for this case, and then think about it all the time. This is your work as manager. Don't shirk.

Use the review for power pellets. How do you review a single individual's performance on a software team that has the characteristics I've been describing? It would seem that a team on which everybody succeeds or fails together would preclude the recognition of outstanding individual achievement and that rewards would have to be tied to team achievement.

But a software career is like a video game in that there are multiple levels demanding increasing degrees of mastery. Everybody on the team is working on some level, trying to get through it and to ascend to the next. Each level produces its unique challenges, and each should be confusing at first, difficult, frightening, and even maddening. The rules differ at each level. Behavior that was successful on one level is ineffective or even disastrous on the next. Gradually, a team member masters the new environment, and then she's thrust into the next.

It's useful to actually identify these levels—to number them, to generally define expected behavior and results for each—and then to help people determine whether they're above, at, or below expectations with respect to their levels. This is the content of a review.

A software career is also like a video game in that players are supplied with multiple "lives" and special "power packs" that enable them to transcend the difficulties at each level in spite of calamities. The place they go to renew their lives or to acquire special power pellets is the review.

The review is an opportunity to reconcile perspectives, uncover the genius, and reset expectations in accordance with short-term potential. Direct, unflinching, and supportive communications are best in the review, although they are the hardest. It's essential that you and the team member come to some agreement (or agree to disagree) on where he or she is in the video game of software development. On what is required to get to the next level. On what from the previous level must be unlearned (though remembered). On what must still be learned at the current level.

Maturation at a given level will take highly individual forms. People have to find their own ways to achieve or transcend the results expected at each level. Basically, each level should require that the team member work within a larger time horizon than at the previous level, that he or she have wider impact and greater leverage, and that he or she show increasing leadership of either more and more people or increasingly effective people. (Don't confuse leadership with supervision.)

An Eclectic List of Resources
for Software Development Leaders

It's hard for me to say precisely where all of the ideas in this book have come from. They've probably come from other books and more than a few of them from other people, many of whom I mentioned in the acknowledgments at the beginning of this book. To give credit where I know it's due in the wider world, though, and to give you some useful (even if obvious) pointers to important ideas and people, I'll make brief mention here of some thinkers, writers, and historical figures I know have had a big impact on my way of thinking and who probably should on yours.

Anyone claiming to be civilized ought to have a basic understanding of Freud. Read something that accurately describes Freud's signal insights: read Freud himself, his correspondence, his biographers, or even the Cliff notes—or watch a movie. Do something about Freud: one way or another, develop an appreciation for our greatest explorer of the psyche. If you can, undergo some sort of psychoanalytic experience. It's expensive, even luxurious, but it can (though it won't necessarily) add an entirely new dimension to your awareness.

Darwin, of course, was our greatest explorer of nature. His discoveries find application all over the place, in ways we haven't even noticed yet. Get a handle on Darwin's perceptions. The effort will pay you back a thousandfold in interpretive if not prescriptive information. Along the same (but more contemporary) lines, check out Richard Dawkins, especially *The Selfish Gene.* Dawkins should get you thinking about the role of evolution in societies.

Spend some time with Shakespeare. It doesn't have to be a lot of time, but the good leader will have a sense of the beauty of symbols and of their power to inspire and lead, and Shakespeare is the absolute best ever at symbol manipulation. (*A Midsummer Night's Dream* is not unlike the software development experience.)

Lincoln, General Grant, and Churchill are leaders who have been especially interesting to me. Grant would have been a great software development manager: he plunged into battle and never let up until the thing was over. And Churchill always rewards study: he had a peculiar genius, he lived by his convictions in spite of widespread resistance to them, and he had a spectacularly inspirational style of leadership, encouraging the Allies to perseverance and victory with the power of his words and a skillful manipulation of symbols. He wrote out his speeches in blank verse! Lincoln combined profound emotional resonance with extreme pragmatism.

Software is a uniquely modern form of expression, and you need to develop a sensitivity to modern modalities. Take a look at the work, the times, the milieu of Picasso. The rest of modern art stems from Picasso. Art goes on at the most extreme boundary of reality. Almost all design, fashion, and other esthetic considerations originate in art and wash over the rest of civilization like an an esthetic wave. Architecture, music, and the other design disciplines also give form to various universal and contemporary impulses. Understand your times.

For esthetic theory, which I discussed only a little in this book, I suggest you read Rudolf Arnheim, especially *Art and Visual Perception,* which will tell you everything you need to know about user interface design and creating products that are compelling.

The most pleasant way to spoonfeed yourself a sense of history is to read Will and Ariel Durant's magnum opus, *The Story of Civilization.* If you're going to create great software, you'll have to engage with the historical dimension, and it's hard to see how you could achieve it without a general awareness of the major movements of civilization.

See the movie *Babette's Feast* as a primer on opening up people's awareness. Much of your time as a leader will be spent in turning people on to richer ways of experiencing things, and this movie is a great parable of that service.

For a true picture of the mission and the dedication of an artist (of a software developer, for example), see the movie *Ed Wood.*

If you don't want to pursue these sources of inspiration, just keep making software. You can't help but get better at it.

Index

Index

corporate software development, 7, 158
creativity
  and change, 169–70
  and group psyche, 50–51, 79
Creators vs. Facilitators, 48
customers
  addressing needs of, 70–78
  captive, 68
  and computer illiteracy, 76–77
  individuals vs. markets, 69
  listening to, 72–73, 74
  and multi-release strategy, 76, 77–78, 164
  purchasing decision stages, 70
  relationships with, 68–78, 164
  and Visual C++, 73–75
customer satisfaction product features, 28

D

Darwin, Charles, 177
Dawkins, Richard, 177
death marches, 33, 89
debugging, 129, 153–55
deliverables
  as commitments, 102, 104–6
  frequency of, 102–6
  and milestones, 116
  movement toward crispness, 127–28
dependencies
  and deliverables, 102, 104–6
  external, 83
development function. *See also* milestones; software
    development projects
  defined, 11, 85
  dimensions of, 87–88
  effective number of people, 39
  end of, 129
  importance of milestones, 114
  jam session analogy, 87–88
  need for visibility in, 102–6
  during opening moves, 87
  as play, 89–91
  team concerns, 43
development organizations. *See also* teams
  Creators vs. Facilitators in, 48

hiring in, 168–70
intellectual vs. mechanical activity in, 5–6
job functions within, 10–11
managing people, 168–75
doctor model, 94–96
documentation function, 11, 43
dogfooding, 125
dumbness perception, 76–77
Durant, Will and Ariel, 178

E

Ed Wood, 178
ease of use, vs. configurability, 69
empathy
  with customers, 71–73
  with team, 13, 15
empowerment
  and consensus, 24, 27, 39, 128
  and feature teams, 40
  and negotiating milestone deliverables, 116
  and scheduling, 88
  overview, 53–55
  and technology plan, 24, 27, 29
endgame
  Beta testing, 153
  bug triage, 129, 153–55
  defined, 7
  focus on shipping, 151–52
esthetics, 71, 79–83, 178
expectations, doctor model, 94–96

F

Facilitators vs. Creators, 48
features
  as propitiation to the software gods, 83
  as triangle element, 88, 96–97, 128–29
  types of, 28–29
feature shoot-outs, 63
feature teams
  and accountability, 40–42

Index

Jim

Jim McCarthy has participated in the creation and shipping of over twenty-five PC software products.

Jim first started programming on a TRS-80 Model I in 1976, with Level I BASIC. Not too long after, he abandoned practically every other interest in life to pursue his growing passion for programming personal computers. A couple of years after his experience with the Trash-80 and BASIC, Jim loaded up a camper with a computer, a BDS C compiler, and books by Kernighan and Ritchie, Plauger, and Knuth and took off for the woods. He stayed in the woods for weeks, working night and day to teach himself "real programming."

The cathode ray tube cast an eerie shadow in the dark forest, and the high-tech hum of the computer made an unearthly sound in the woods.

Jim went on to start his own one-man shop and later to work at AT&T Bell Laboratories, the Whitewater Group, and Microsoft Corporation. He is currently a director in the Visual C++ Business Unit at Microsoft. Although he delivers software development seminars and talks throughout the world, Jim is still developing and shipping commercial software for a living, and he says he is not yet a burnt-out case.

Maybe that's because Jim also paints, writes, raises children, and sculpts stone and wood in a log house on Crystal Lake in the state of Washington.

On occasion, his CRT still illuminates the woods.

To contact Jim about the ideas he presents in this book, e-mail jimmcc@microsoft.com.

You can reach Patrick McCarthy at Pfm77@aol.com.

The manuscript for this book was prepared and submitted to Microsoft Press in electronic form. Text files were prepared using Microsoft Word 6 for Windows. Pages were composed by designLab using PageMaker 5.0 for the Macintosh, with text in Caslon and display type in Caslon Italic. Composed pages were delivered to the printer as electronic prepress files.

Cover Design
Rebecca Geisler

Cover/Interior Artist
Patrick McCarthy

Interior Graphic Designers
Kim Eggleston
Amy Peppler Adams, designLab

Layout Artists
designLab —
    C. Douglas Lathom
    Amy Peppler Adams

Proofreader/Copy Editor
Shawn Peck

Indexer
Julie Kawabata

Software Development
Jolt Excellence Award, 1994

Code Complete
by Steve McConnell

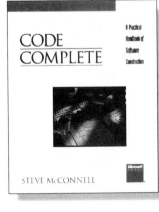

ISBN 1-55615-484-4
880 pages
$35.00 ($44.95 Canada)

This bestselling practical handbook of software construction covers the art and science of software implementation, from design to testing. Examples are provided in C, Pascal, Basic, FORTRAN, and Ada—but the focus is on programming techniques.

Topics include:

- up-front planning
- applying good design techniques to construction
- using data effectively
- managing construction activities
- reviewing for errors
- relating personal character to superior software

Critical Praise for *Code Complete*

"Microsoft Press has published what I consider to be the definitive book on software construction. This is a book that belongs on every software developer's bookshelf. McConnell has made a tremendous contribution to software development literature."

—Warren Keuffel, *Software Development*

"Every half an age or so, you come across a book that short circuits the school of experience and saves you years of purgatory. I cannot adequately express how good this book really is...a work of brilliance."

—Jeff Dunteman, *PC Techniques*

"If you are or aspire to be a professional programmer, this may be the wisest $35 investment you'll ever make. McConnell's stated purpose is to narrow the gap between the knowledge of industry gurus and common commercial practice. The amazing thing is that he succeeds."

—*IEEE Micro*

Microsoft Press

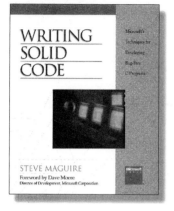

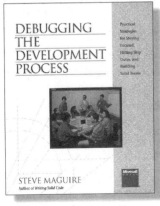

Register Today!

Return this
Dynamics of Software Development
registration card for:

✔ a Microsoft Press® catalog

✔ exclusive offers on specially
  priced books

1-55615-823-8A   *Dynamics of Software Development*   *Owner Registration Card*

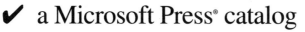

_____

NAME

_____

INSTITUTION OR COMPANY NAME

_____

ADDRESS

_____

_____

CITY   STATE   ZIP

Quality Computer Books

For a free catalog of
Microsoft Press® products, call
1-800-MSPRESS